A Souvenir of

The Royal Wedding

A Souvenir of
The Royal Wedding

Lornie Leete-Hodge

Optimum Books

Photographic acknowledgments
The illustrations on the following pages are reproduced by Gracious Permission of Her Majesty The Queen: 76, 77 top, 80-81, 139 bottom, 140 top, 140 bottom, 148 top.

Associated Newspapers, London 45 bottom, 114 bottom, 129 bottom; BBC Hulton Picture Library, London 60 top, 60 centre, 60 bottom, 61 top, 61 bottom left, 61 bottom right, 63 bottom, 78 bottom, 81, 83 top, 87 bottom, 88 top, 89 top, 89 bottom, 100 bottom, 122 bottom, 156 bottom right; Central Press, London 9 top, 10 left, 15 bottom, 20 bottom, 22, 30 bottom, 31 bottom, 35 bottom, 36 top, 38 top, 38 bottom, 41, 42 top, 46 top, 64 top, 70 top, 91 bottom left, 93 top left, 119 top, 138, 144 top, 152 top, 154 bottom, 159 top; Epoque, London 48 top; Fox Photos, London 8; Tim Graham, London 6, 37, 42 bottom right, 43 top, 43 bottom, 44, 45 top, 46 bottom, 47, 48 bottom left, 48 bottom right, 49, 50 bottom, 51, 52 top, 52 bottom left, 52 bottom right, 53 top, 53 centre, 63 top, 66 bottom, 68, 71, 72 top, 72 bottom, 73 top, 74 top, 74 bottom left, 74 bottom right, 75, 96 bottom, 99 top, 117, 137, 139 top, 143 top, 145, 146 bottom, 147, 157 bottom; Hamlyn Group Picture Library 12 bottom, 58, 64 centre, 64 bottom, 79, 83 bottom left, 87 top, 88 bottom, 90 bottom, 93 top right, 125 top, 125 bottom, 141, 142 top, 142 bottom, 148 bottom, 152 bottom, 158, 159 bottom left; Keystone Press Agency, London 11, 19, 23 top, 24 top, 25, 26 top, 26 bottom, 27, 29 top, 31 top, 32, 33, 35 top, 36 bottom, 38 centre, 39 top, 40 top, 40 bottom, 50 top, 53 bottom, 56 bottom right, 62 left, 70 bottom, 84 bottom, 85, 90 top, 91 top, 91 bottom right, 92 top left, 92 top right, 93 bottom, 94 top, 95 top, 96 top, 99 bottom left, 99 bottom right, 100 top, 101 top, 104–105, 106 top left, 107 top, 108 top, 108 bottom, 110 top, 111 top, 113 top, 113 bottom, 114 top, 115 top, 115 bottom, 116 top, 116 bottom, 118 right, 119 bottom, 120-121, 122 top left, 124, 126 bottom, 127, 128, 129 top, 130 top, 131 top, 133 top, 135 bottom, 148 centre, 150 centre, 150 bottom, 151, 154 top, 157 top, 160 top; Serge Lemoine, London 103 top; Ministry of Defence 28 bottom, 29 bottom, 30 top, 110 bottom left; National Army Museum, London 77 bottom; National Portrait Gallery, London 59, 65; Photographers International, Chilworth 69 top; Popperfoto, London 9 bottom, 10 right, 12 top, 13, 14, 16 top, 16 bottom, 17, 18 top right, 18 bottom, 20 top, 21, 23 bottom, 28 top, 34, 39 bottom, 42 bottom left, 56 top, 56 bottom left, 80, 83 bottom right, 84 top, 86, 92 bottom, 133 bottom, 144 bottom, 146 top, 148-149, 155 top, 155 centre, 155 bottom, 156 bottom left; Press Association, London 54 left, 55 top, 55 bottom, 57 left, 57 right, 66 top left, 66 top right, 67 top, 67 bottom, 94 bottom, 131 bottom, 159 bottom right; Sport and General Press Agency, London 102 bottom, 106 top right, 143 bottom, 150 top; Syndication International, London 15 top, 18 top left, 54 right, 62 right, 69 bottom, 73 bottom, 82, 94 centre, 95 bottom, 97 left, 97 right, 98 top, 98 bottom, 101 bottom, 102 top, 103 bottom, 106 bottom, 107 bottom, 109, 110 bottom left, 111 bottom, 112 top, 118 left, 122 top right, 123, 130 bottom, 132, 134, 135 top, 136, 153 top, 153 bottom, 156 top; Times, London 112 bottom, 126 top; Victoria and Albert Museum, London 78 top left, 78 top right.

Designed by Groom & Pickerill

This edition published by Optimum Books 1981
Reprinted 1981

Prepared by
The Hamlyn Publishing Group Limited
London · New York · Sydney · Toronto
Astronaut House, Feltham, Middlesex, England

Copyright © The Hamlyn Publishing Group Limited 1981
ISBN 0 600 37811 X

Printed in England

Contents

The Engagement

'It is with the greatest pleasure that The Queen and The Duke of Edinburgh announce the betrothal of their beloved son, The Prince of Wales, to the Lady Diana Spencer, daughter of the Earl Spencer and the Honourable Mrs Shand Kydd.'

So read the official announcement made at Buckingham Palace at precisely eleven o'clock on the morning of 24 February 1981.

The speculation was over, and it was a happy time. Outside the Palace the photographers and newsmen were hurrying down the Mall, eager not to miss a crumb of information. The telephone and telegraph wires sizzled.

For years the world's most eligible bachelor had been in the headlines. The Prince himself had once said thirty was a good age at which to marry, but when he reached, and passed, that time and no announcement had been made, the disappointed press and public sat back to wait and continue the game of speculation.

Rumours grew more rife when, in 1980, the Prince bought a house in Gloucestershire, near to his sister, Princess Anne. Highgrove, purchased from publisher MP, Maurice Macmillan, is just right for a young royal couple, with thirty rooms and extensive parkland. The house is in the heart of the Beaufort Hunt country, so the Prince will be able to enjoy his hunting, and there is easy access to London and the polo grounds of Cirencester and Windsor. Highgrove is, first and foremost, a lovely home, and obviously one that appealed to a family-loving man such as the Prince of Wales, who, perhaps instinctively, knew that this would be the right place to begin the adventure of married life.

At the Palace on the morning of 24 February it was business as usual. The clouds had lifted and a pale wintry sun broke through to cast its light across the Royal Standard fluttering at the masthead. Inside, preparations were being completed with the usual Palace efficiency for an Investiture, one of the fourteen or so held throughout the year. The men and women who were to receive decorations from the Queen in recognition of their services to the nation were gathered in the Ball Room with members of their families.

On this day there was a very slight difference to the usual Palace routine. After the Queen had entered, preceded by her Bodyguard of the Yeomen of the Guard, the Lord Chamberlain told those waiting that Her Majesty had asked him to read an official announcement. As the news of the engagement was given, spontaneous applause broke out. Obviously delighted to share her happiness with her subjects, the Queen then proceeded with the Investiture.

Following tradition, the Prince and Lady Diana appeared together in the grounds of Buckingham Palace after lunching with the Queen and the rest of the Royal Family that day. Lady Diana, smiling happily, posed with her fiancé and showed her lovely sapphire and diamond ring for the cameras. Then came a break with tradition. The newly engaged and delighted couple answered a barrage of questions from the media in front of the television cameras. Laughing and smiling, the Prince admitted that he had wondered if Lady Diana would accept him, and Lady Diana, without a trace of hesitation, said that she had had no doubts at all.

The Prince of Wales was known to the whole world and admired by all. Now it was the turn of his chosen bride to be introduced to the people and to win equal love and respect from those whose queen she will one day be.

Prince Charles: a Portrait

When Prince Charles Philip Arthur George, eldest son of Her Majesty Queen Elizabeth II and Prince Philip, was born at Buckingham Palace on 14 November 1948 there was great rejoicing and the floodlights in Trafalgar Square were turned to blue to indicate that the child was a prince.

The new baby was christened in the Music Room of the Palace on 15 December 1948, in a robe designed by Prince Albert for Queen Victoria's firstborn. The Lily Font, also designed by Prince Albert, was brought from Windsor for the occasion and, following a tradition dating from the time of the Crusades, holy water from the River Jordan was used by Dr Geoffrey Fisher, the Archbishop of Canterbury, for the baptism.

Amongst the child's eight godparents were his grandparents, King George VI and Queen

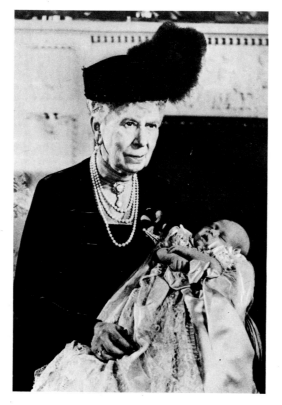

A proud great-grandmother, and the last Princess of Wales, Queen Mary holds Prince Charles, future Prince of Wales, after his christening. He is wearing the robe designed by Prince Albert.

Elizabeth, his aunt, Princess Margaret, and Prince Philip's cousin (and Lord Mountbatten's eldest daughter), then Lady Brabourne. Princess Margaret, acting as proxy for King Haakon of Norway who was unable to attend, handed the baby to the Archbishop. The organist of the Chapel Royal played Handel's *Water Music*.

Among the christening presents was a silver-gilt cup and cover from Queen Mary which George III had given to a godson in 1780. She noted in her diary that she 'gave a present from my great grandfather, to my great grandson 168 years later'.

In 1949 the Prince and his parents took up residence in Clarence House, not far from Buckingham Palace, and the infant was often seen in nearby St James's Park or Green Park in an ordinary pram on outings with his nanny. In 1950 Princess Anne was born at Clarence House, and with his sister the Prince learned discipline from an early age. At the time, the Duke of Edinburgh was still a serving naval officer in Malta, and Princess Elizabeth often flew there to see him, leaving her children in the care of her parents. By 1951, however, the King's health had worsened and the Duke of Edinburgh felt obliged to give up command of HMS *Magpie* in order to assist with increasing royal duties on behalf of his father-in-law.

In January 1952 Princess Elizabeth and her husband set off on a tour of East Africa, Australia and New Zealand. They had got no further than Treetops Hotel in Kenya when, on 6 February, King George VI died and the new queen had to return home with her husband to take up the duties of monarchy.

The three-year-old Prince Charles was waiting at Clarence House on 7 February when his parents came home, and from that moment his life changed. The first male in direct succession for more than fifteen years, he was trained from babyhood for the role of

A Cecil Beaton portrait of Princess Elizabeth and her young son in November 1948.

The birth certificate of a prince.

492	Fourteenth November 1948 Buckingham Palace	Charles Philip Arthur George	Boy	His Royal Highness Philip. Duke of Edinburgh	Her Royal Highness The Princess Elizabeth Alexandra Mary, Duchess of Edinburgh	His Royal Highness The Duke of Edinburgh (Lieutenant, R.N)	Philip Father Buckingham Palace, S.W.1	Fifteenth December, 1948	I. L. Mare Registrar
493									

Above: Prince Charles enjoying an outing in the park with his nanny on his second birthday.

Above right: Prince Charles accompanies his mother and Princess Anne as they catch the train for a holiday at Balmoral in 1950. This was Princess Anne's first public appearance.

king that it was his destiny to play. As Heir Apparent, he was now also Duke of Cornwall, Duke of Rothesay, Earl of Carrick, Baron of Renfrew, Lord of the Isles and Great Steward of Scotland.

The Queen and the Duke of Edinburgh moved back into Buckingham Palace with their family, and the Queen Mother moved into their old home at Clarence House. On 2 June 1953, when Prince Charles was four and a half years old, he watched his mother's coronation service from the royal box at Westminster Abbey with his grandmother, the Queen Mother, and his aunt, Princess Margaret. As Duke of Cornwall, senior royal duke and head of the peerage, Prince Charles should have taken an oath of allegiance to his mother, but in view of his age this was postponed.

In November the Queen and her husband set off on a six months' tour of the Commonwealth, basically the round-the-world trip her father's death had cut short, but with a much-extended itinerary. The Royal Yacht *Britannia*, launched in April, was still undergoing trials, so they flew to Jamaica to join a converted cruise liner, the *Gothic*, planning to link up with *Britannia* on the way home. In the spring of the following year Prince Charles and Princess Anne, on their first overseas trip, sailed in the Royal Yacht to Malta, where their great-uncle, Lord Louis Mountbatten, was based as Commander-in-Chief, Mediterranean Fleet. At Tobruk the Queen and Prince Philip were piped aboard *Britannia* to join their children for the trip home via Gibraltar. The yacht sailed up the Thames to the Pool of London, and in a stately barge the

Gallant, even at the age of five, Prince Charles gives his sister a helping hand down the steps of the Cathedral in Malta. It was the children's first overseas trip and they were on their way to meet their parents at the end of the 1953-54 Commonwealth Tour.

Royal Family continued a triumphant progress, with the Prime Minister, Sir Winston Churchill, aboard to share in the welcome.

Prince Charles now had teachers for daily lessons at the Palace, and his education was enhanced by visits to the Tower of London and Madame Tussaud's, as well as to museums and other places of interest. He was taught music and dancing and joined other boys in a private gymnasium.

Following his education at the Palace, the Prince spent two terms at Hill House, a private day school in London. With his arrival in January 1957 he made British history by becoming the first Heir Apparent ever to be a schoolboy. The headmaster had warned the other pupils not to fuss him, so the Prince had no special privileges and gradually adapted to the new regime. In his first term he took part

in the school's Field Day, as it was called, with his parents and sister watching. In the summer, before starting at a new school, the Prince had his tonsils removed and went down to Holkham Hall in Norfolk to convalesce.

The school which Prince Charles went to as a boarder in 1957 was Cheam, a preparatory school in Berkshire where his father had been enrolled twenty-seven years earlier. The school, which claims to be England's oldest preparatory one, had a distinguished roll of former pupils, including a Prime Minister, Henry Addington, later Viscount Sidmouth, Lord Hardinge of Penshurst, Sir Iain Hamilton of Gallipoli fame, and Lord Randolph Churchill, father of Sir Winston.

The Queen and the Duke of Edinburgh accompanied their son when he joined the school, and he was immediately surrounded

Right: Getting acquainted with the famous apes at Gibraltar.

Below: A charming third-birthday picture of Prince Charles with his grandfather, King George VI.

by a blaze of publicity, not helped by the presence of his private detective.

While he was still at Cheam the Queen announced, on 26 July 1958, that she was creating Prince Charles Prince of Wales. Until that time he had officially been known as the Duke of Cornwall, a title to which the eldest son of a sovereign automatically succeeds in accordance with a charter of 1337. The title of Prince of Wales had to be conferred by letters patent and is held until the Prince becomes king; it is not inherited by an heir. The announcement was made at the Commonwealth Games in Cardiff, opened by the Duke of Edinburgh as the Queen was ill. He introduced her recorded message announcing that 'I intend to create my son Charles, Prince of Wales today. When he is grown up I will present him to you at Caernarvon.'

In 1960 Princess Margaret announced her engagement to Antony Armstrong-Jones, who was to become Earl of Snowdon and Constable of Caernarvon Castle, and there was another addition to the Royal Family with the birth of Prince Andrew. Prince Edward's birth was to follow in 1964.

At school Prince Charles became captain of his soccer XI and acted the part of Richard III in *The Last Baron*, showing his early liking for the stage. He also developed his talents as a pianist and a painter.

In May 1962 the Prince again found himself following in his father's footsteps when he entered Gordonstoun. The school, on the shores of the Moray Firth, offered a rigorous, exciting existence, and the Prince quickly learned how to look after himself. The syllabus included many games periods and training in special activities such as estate work and seamanship. There was training also in community service—sea and army cadets, fire service, Scouts and coastguard duties, as well as life-saving and mountain rescue. Prince Charles trained with the sea cadets and won bronze and silver medals in the Duke of Edinburgh Award Scheme set up by his father. Physical fitness became almost a cult, and even today the Prince attaches extreme importance to good health.

Gordonstoun is situated near to Balmoral, and Prince Charles spent much of his leisure time with his grandmother, the Queen Mother, at her house at Birkhall on the estate, joining her on many fishing expeditions. He had the opportunity to try his hand at another sport in 1963, when he went to Tarasp in Switzerland to join Prince Ludwig of Hesse on a winter sports holiday. Prince Charles eventually became a very proficient skier and goes to Switzerland regularly each winter to enjoy the sport.

Prince Charles dressed for the coronation of his mother in 1953.

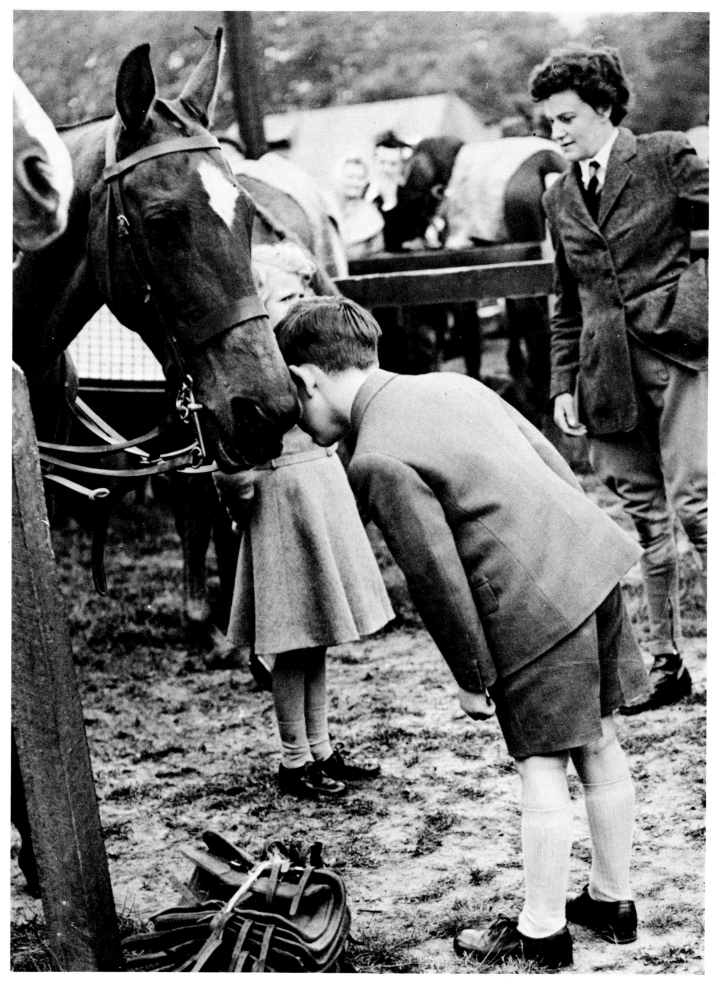

Top left: The new pupil, Prince Charles, greeting his headmaster at Cheam School on his arrival in 1957.

Bottom left: Prince Charles performs a balancing act at Hill House's Field Day in 1957.

Right: Escorting his mother and grandmother on their way to Princess Margaret's wedding in 1960.

Below: Cecil Beaton has captured Prince Charles's delight in his new brother, Prince Andrew.

Facing page: A prince and princess enjoying the dodgems with Lady Anne Nevill and a circus official after a visit to the Bertram Mills Circus at Olympia in 1959.

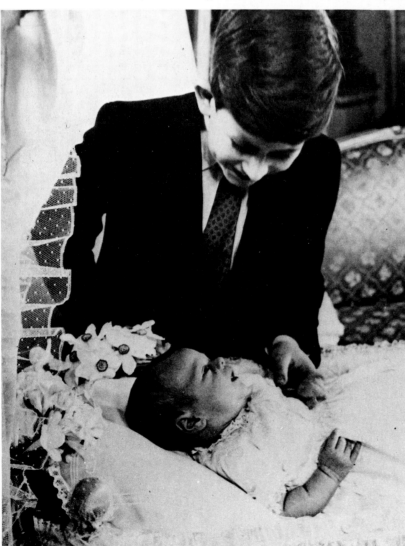

Already a keen sailor in the school yacht, *Pinta*, and on board *Coweslip* with his father at Cowes, the Prince had a taste of the real naval life to come when he visited HMS *Vernon*, the Navy's training camp at Portsmouth. But his interests were musical as well as military and sporting, and after hearing Jacqueline Dupré playing the cello at the Festival Hall he decided to take up the instrument himself.

Meanwhile the Prince was gradually appearing more and more in public. He attended Princess Alexandra's wedding at Westminster Abbey in 1963, and King Constantine's in Athens the following year. At the Greek wedding he was one of the ten people chosen to hold the crowns over the couple's heads during the ceremony.

State occasions began to creep into his programme, and he attended, with his parents, the State Funeral of Sir Winston Churchill at St Paul's Cathedral in 1965. Later that year he was present at a royal garden party at the Palace of Holyroodhouse in Edinburgh, meeting many Scottish and Commonwealth students there.

When Sir Robert Menzies, then Prime Minister of Australia, came to England in 1965 the Queen announced that she intended to honour the promise made during her coronation tour of that country 'to send my eldest son to visit you when he is older', and arrangements were made for Prince Charles to go to an Australian public school, Geelong,

Right: Complete with cello, Prince Charles arrives at St Giles' Cathedral in Edinburgh during his time at Gordonstoun.

Far right: Prince Charles leads the way on the Swiss ski slopes.

Below: In 1964 Prince Charles was in Athens to attend the wedding of his second cousin, King Constantine of Greece, and Princess Anne-Marie of Denmark.

near Melbourne. His six months there were to be spent at its country outpost, Timbertop. So, in January 1966, at the age of seventeen, the Prince flew to a new experience on the other side of the world, accompanied by Squadron-Leader David Checketts, an Equerry to Prince Philip who was later to become Prince Charles's first Private Secretary. The Queen Mother happened to be on a visit to Australia during the Prince's first term, so she was able to spend time with him and report on his progress to the Queen and Prince Philip.

While at Geelong, Prince Charles joined the other boys on an annual visit to missionary stations in Papua New Guinea, and he returned home by way of Tahiti, Mexico City and Jamaica, where he joined his parents and sister at the Commonwealth Games, much enriched by his Australian experience.

After his return to Britain there was a final year to be completed at Gordonstoun, during which he became Guardian, or head boy, and in November 1966 legally came of age at eighteen. In July 1967 he gained his A-levels in History and French, and arrangements were made for him to study Archaeology and Physical and Social Anthropology at Trinity College, Cambridge, where King Edward VII, King George VI and the Duke of Gloucester had all been students.

In October 1967, having been greeted on his arrival in a red Mini by the Master of Trinity, Lord Butler of Saffron Walden, the Prince took up residence at Cambridge. He

lived in college, competing for his degree on an equal basis with other students. He joined an amateur theatrical group, the Dryden Society, and the university polo team, winning a half-blue and scoring the only goal in the game against Oxford in 1969. In a Trinity revue he was given a great reception when, complete with bin, he appeared as the dustman whom he had earlier said had disturbed him by singing!

In 1967 the Prince, with his sister, took part in the State Opening of Parliament for the first time, less than a month before he celebrated his nineteenth birthday at Trinity. Towards the end of the year he was back in Australia again, but only for a few hours, in order to represent the Queen at the memorial service for the former Prime Minister, Harold Holt, who had been drowned at sea.

Gradually, the Prince was emerging more into public life. The date for his investiture as Prince of Wales had been set for 1 July 1969, and the Earl Marshal, the sixteenth Duke of Norfolk, was planning the ceremonial, to take place against a setting designed by Lord Snowdon.

Meanwhile there was another ancient title for the Prince to assume, and on 17 June 1968 he was installed as a Knight of the Garter at Windsor Castle. The ceremony began with his investiture, when the Queen, watched only by the Knights and Officers of the Order, invested Prince Charles with its insignia of garter, riband, star and collar. Lunch in the Waterloo Chamber of the Castle followed, then the procession to St George's Chapel where, with age-old ritual, the Prince was installed, acquiring a stall on the north side of the aisle.

Having stepped back into the past for this day of ceremonial, the Prince was plunged back into the twentieth century when, as a member of the Cambridge University Air Squadron, he began flying in the summer of 1968, thus fulfilling a childhood ambition. He went on to make his first solo flight in January 1969, further emulating his father, who is an experienced pilot.

The 'Sailor Prince' enjoying himself on Coweslip *at Cowes in 1971.*

With the day of the Investiture drawing nearer and public interest in the Royal Family ever growing, the BBC was given permission to make a film showing a typical year of royal activities. It was produced by Richard Cawston, who spent seventy-five days filming members of the Royal Family in various locations and moods, serious at some important ceremony perhaps or happily relaxing at a family picnic at Balmoral. Among the many people who appeared in the film was the American President at the time, Richard Nixon, who joked with Prince Charles about television appearances. This particular appearance by the Queen and her family revealed them to the public in a light never before imagined, and *Royal Family* proved extremely popular. Radio interviews with Prince Charles followed, the first on St David's Day in 1969, and he was later in the year interviewed on television for the first time.

Before his investiture Prince Charles spent a term at the University College of Wales at Aberystwyth, with the primary intention of learning Welsh. After a little initial reluctance the other students accepted him, and he worked hard at mastering the intricacies of the language, assisted by the university's language laboratory. While at Aberystwyth, he addressed the Youth Eisteddfod, speaking

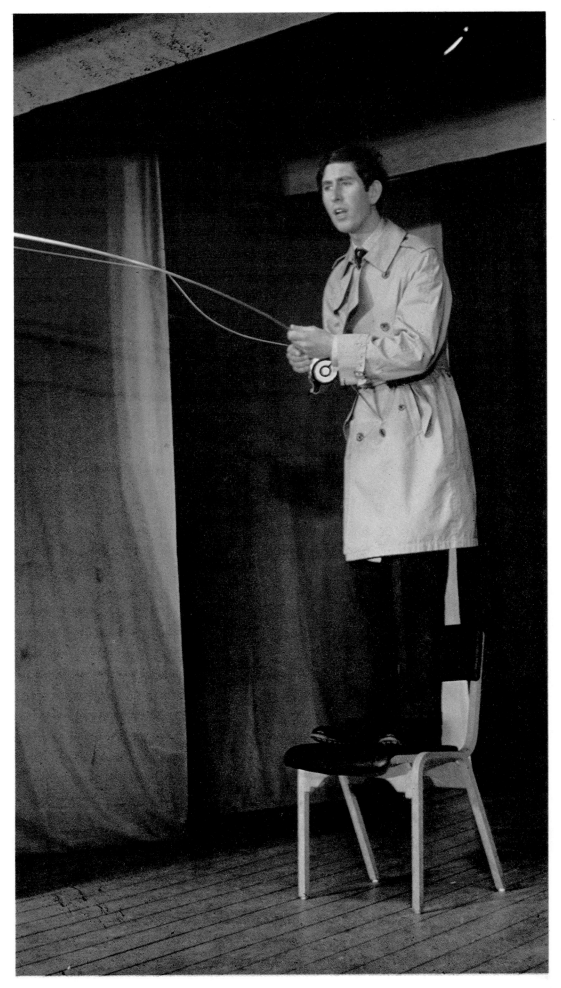

*The 'Actor Prince' in a
Cambridge University revue
in 1969.*

fluent Welsh which gave great pleasure to his audience.

At about this time the Welsh Regiment and the South Wales Borderers had been merged to form the new Royal Regiment of Wales, and in June 1969 Prince Charles, as their Colonel-in-Chief, took the salute at the inauguration parade at Cardiff Castle, wearing on his military uniform the riband and star of the Garter and the Coronation Medal awarded in 1953. He presented new colours to the regiment and accepted the Freedom of the City of Cardiff on behalf of his soldiers, again delighting everyone by speaking in Welsh at an official luncheon.

And so to the Investiture itself. It took place at a time when many new and exciting events were fascinating the world – the space probes and the first flight of Concorde, to name but the most dramatic – but to the British, and to the Welsh in particular, the enactment of this ancient ceremony was all-important. A special stamp was designed to commemorate the event, and the Welsh turned out in their thousands to welcome their new Prince. A major occasion in every sense, it was for the Queen's eldest son a very meaningful ceremony and a step forward in the natural progression of an heir to the throne.

The Investiture took place on 1 July 1969 at Caernarvon Castle, a splendid setting for the enactment of this age-old ritual. The invited guests numbered four thousand but, with colour television a recent development, there was likely to be an audience of something like

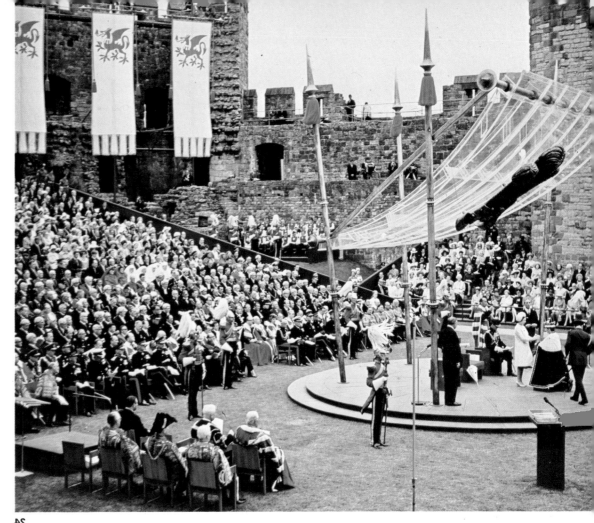

Right: Lord Snowdon's design for the Investiture ceremony is shown to great effect against the background of Caernarvon Castle.

Below: The Investiture procession wends its way at Caernarvon on 1 July 1969.

five hundred million. Lord Snowdon had already played a vital role by designing a platform that would most effectively enhance the open-air ceremony and stand up well to the scrutiny of television cameras.

Before an audience composed of mayors, sheriffs, members of parliament, peers and representatives of Welsh youth, the Queen walked in procession to her place on the dais. Once there, she commanded the Duke of Norfolk to direct Garter King of Arms to fetch the Prince. From the Chamberlain Tower where he had been waiting he was led with his sponsors in procession to the dais, preceded by heralds, Garter King of Arms and the Secretary of State for Wales, and followed by peers carrying the regalia.

The Queen then proceeded to invest her eldest son with the coronet, rod (symbolizing temporal rule), ring, sword and mantle of his office. The specially designed coronet weighed 105 ounces (2977g) and was made of 24-carat gold set with gems. It was the work of Louis Osman and was presented by the Goldsmiths' Company of London.

Prince Charles, wearing the uniform of the Royal Regiment of Wales, knelt and did homage to the Queen, with the words: 'I, Charles, Prince of Wales, do become your liege man of life and limb and of earthly worship, and faith and truth I will bear unto

The Queen crowns her kneeling son Prince of Wales with the coronet of gold made specially for the occasion.

you to live and die against all manner of folks.' He then exchanged the Kiss of Fealty with his mother and listened to a loyal address, to which he replied, partly in Welsh. There followed a religious service, after which the Queen presented the Prince to the people of Wales at the Queen's Gate, the King's Gate and the platform facing the Lower Ward of the Castle. The scene must have had particular poignancy for Prince Charles's great-uncle, then Duke of Windsor, who had himself been invested as Prince of Wales at Caernarvon in 1911, and who watched the 1969 Investiture on television at his home in Paris.

The new Prince of Wales spent four days touring the Principality, visiting many towns in both north and south and travelling part of the way on the Royal Yacht *Britannia*. An outdoor pursuits centre, an agricultural college and a school were all on his itinerary, and at Cardiff he was given the Freedom of the City.

All the pomp and pageantry usually associated with Great Britain were present at the Investiture of Prince Charles, which was a timely and powerful reminder of his inheritance and his duty. The ceremony, with all its outward show, was essentially one of commitment rather than ritual, and it was, for all, a very moving occasion, one long to be remembered.

The motto of the Prince of Wales is '*Ich Dien*', meaning 'I Serve', and it is one which he has endeavoured to make a reality. There

Right: Followed by his sister, Prince Charles arrives for lunch at the Mansion House after receiving the Freedom of the City of London at Guildhall in 1971.

Below: On safari in Kenya with Princess Anne in 1971, the Prince is greeted at Lake Rudolf with a tribal dance of welcome.

can be no prince who has tried more faithfully to serve his country, without thought for himself, than Prince Charles. He is justly proud of his past and looks to his future with confidence. At his investiture he remarked that 'the past can be just as much a stimulus to the future as anything else'.

After his investiture as Prince of Wales, Prince Charles continued to take a lively interest in Wales and its people, whom he visits regularly. He was Chairman of the Steering Committee for Wales 'Countryside in 1970' Conference and became President of the Welsh Environment Foundation in 1971. As its Colonel-in-Chief he inspects the Royal Regiment of Wales from time to time, and when he paid a visit to the Federal Republic of Germany in February 1971 he did not forget the regiment at Osnabrück.

It was Prince Charles's twenty-first birthday on 14 November 1969, and his fellow students at Trinity College marked the occasion by placing a 300-foot banner with the words 'Happy Birthday, Charles' between the towers of the dining hall and the college chapel. On a more serious note, the Prince attended a special private service of Holy Communion at the Tower of London. Here he made an act of thanksgiving and dedicated his future life as Heir to the Throne. This private act was in contrast to the public broadcast made by his mother in 1947 on her twenty-first birthday.

In the evening there was a celebration party at Buckingham Palace, when the Prince's love of music was indulged by a special concert at which Yehudi Menuhin played. (Again there is a contrast, but this time with the celebrations planned by Prince Andrew for his twenty-first birthday party in 1981. At these the star performer was Elton John.) University friends mingled with kings and queens, who included King Olav of Norway and King Constantine of Greece, and the evening ended in a blaze of light with a firework display.

The new decade of the 1970s started busily for the Prince. He found himself not only very much caught up in a life of public service but also making a number of new beginnings.

On 11 February 1970, wearing parliamentary robes and the collar of the Order of the Garter, Prince Charles entered the House of Lords behind a small procession led by Black Rod and followed by Garter King of Arms, the Earl Marshal, the Lord Great Chamberlain, the Lord Privy Seal, the Lord President of the Council and a man bearing his coronet on a cushion. Beside the Prince were his two sponsors, the Duke of Kent and the Duke of Beaufort, for the Prince was there to be formally introduced to the House. He took the age-old Oath of Allegiance to the Queen, then disrobed and, wearing an ordinary suit, listened to a debate in the Chamber.

Prince Charles's final months at Cambridge were very busy for, in addition to his studies, he was called upon to visit Australia and New Zealand with his parents to celebrate the 200th anniversary of Captain Cook's voyage. He went on to Japan alone, returning to Cambridge barely a month before his Finals.

In June 1970 it was announced that Prince Charles had obtained a BA honours degree in History, and the following month he was off on a tour of Canada and the United States, in which he was joined by Princess Anne. The two of them paid a three-day visit to President Nixon in Washington and again met the President's daughter Tricia, who had been a guest at the Prince's Investiture at Caernarvon Castle in the previous year. Americans were

Seen here with his sponsors, the Dukes of Kent and Beaufort, Prince Charles took his seat in the House of Lords in 1970.

Right: August 1971. The Prince receives his wings from Air Chief Marshal Sir Denis Spotswood at Cranwell.

Below: Prince Charles getting the 'hang' of his parachute in July 1971 before making a jump over the English Channel.

impressed by the Prince's knowledge of their history, and for one of his tours the Prince had Gerald Ford, the next President, as his guide.

In the spring of the following year the Prince and his sister were again abroad, this time for a short visit to Kenya. Back at home, the Prince was made a Freeman of the City of London, and preparations began for his service career. On 8 March 1971 he flew to RAF Cranwell to start a five months' course, during which he made his first solo jet flight in a Jet Provost.

On 28 July 1971 the Prince was seen tackling another obstacle with his usual verve and energy. He jumped from an RAF Andover aircraft at 1200 feet (365·76 m), making a successful parachute landing at Studland Bay in Dorset. He had previously undergone preparatory training exercises at the RAF Parachute Training School at Abingdon.

Passing-out day was 20 August 1971 and the Prince received his wings from Air Chief Marshal Sir Denis Spotswood. In October he joined the Royal Naval College, Dartmouth, for a six-week graduate course. This was another step along the traditional road of royal life, trodden by his father, grandfather, great-grandfather and great-uncle before him. Having completed the course, he saw service on board HMS *Norfolk*, a guided-missile destroyer based in Gibraltar, and had twenty-four hours on board a submarine which enabled him to sample conditions 60 feet (18·3 m) under water.

A family bereavement in the death of his great-uncle, the Duke of Windsor, on 28 May 1972 meant that he had to return home from Malta to attend the funeral in St George's Chapel, Windsor. He then returned to his ship, which the Queen later visited when it was berthed at Portsmouth, and afterwards took courses at the Royal Naval Signals School in Hampshire, HMS *Mercury*. He had a happy break for the wedding of Prince Richard of Gloucester in Northamptonshire, though this was sadly to be followed by the death of Prince William of Gloucester a few weeks later.

In November 1972 the Queen and Prince Philip celebrated their Silver Wedding Anniversary with a service of thanksgiving at Westminster Abbey and a lunch at Guildhall

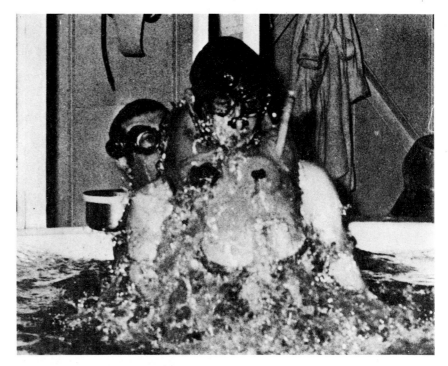

Above: Prince Charles surfacing after making a free buoyant ascent in the submarine escape training tank at HMS Dolphin *at Gosport in 1972.*

Left: 'Action Man' enjoying his favourite sport of polo.

29

Right: On board HMS Minerva in 1973, the ship's assistant navigation officer looks out over the Caribbean to the Virgin Islands.

Below: The Duke of Cornwall leaving Launceston Castle in November 1973, after receiving his 'feudal dues' of a load of firewood, a grey cloak, 100 old shillings, a pound of pepper, a hunting bow, a pair of gilt spurs, a pound of herbs, a salmon spear, a pair of falconer's gauntlets and two greyhounds.

which Prince Charles attended. In the evening he and Princess Anne organized a special party for their parents at which the English Chamber Orchestra played the Wedding March and the Bach Choir sang anthems from the 1947 wedding service.

Prince Charles had not meanwhile neglected his flying interests, having returned to RAF Cranwell for a refresher course, but for the time being the Navy's demands were paramount. He served with a coastal minesweeper and was eventually promoted to Acting Lieutenant on 1 May 1973. That year saw the engagement of Princess Anne to Captain Mark Phillips and their marriage in Westminster Abbey on Prince Charles's twenty-fifth birthday.

Between naval duties the Prince represented the Queen at the independence celebrations in the Bahamas in July 1973, and while his ship was in Australian waters early the next year he was able to join the Royal Family in New Zealand for the Commonwealth Games.

The Duke of Gloucester died in June 1974 and a few days later Prince Charles, still in official mourning, became an Elder Brother of Trinity House. His maiden speech in the House of Lords, made in the same year, was a sixteen-minute one calling for the better co-ordination of leisure facilities.

In September the Prince enrolled in a helicopter training course at the Royal Naval Air Station at Yeovilton, which culminated in his passing out as a fully qualified helicopter pilot and winning the Double Diamond Award for the trainee who had made the most progress. On his squadron's tenth anniversary he led a celebratory fly-past with his personal standard streaming from the winch wire of his aircraft.

At the beginning of 1975 Prince Charles underwent the rigours of a commando training course at the Royal Marine School at Lympstone in Devon, and around the same time he was appointed to HMS *Hermes* as a helicopter pilot. Later in the year he went on a lieutenant's course at the Royal Naval College, Greenwich, following this with a mine warfare course at HMS *Vernon*. His army connections were meanwhile strengthened when he succeeded his father as Colonel of the Welsh Guards.

Prince Charles took command of the minehunter HMS *Bronington* on 9 February 1976 at Rosyth. The ship was nicknamed 'Old Quarter-past-eleven' because her pennant number was 1115. On board ship the Prince grew a beard which was much commented on when he was on leave during the Badminton Horse Trials and did some stewarding. By June he was clean-shaven again. Prince Philip took tea on board the *Bronington* soon after his

With Prince Philip and the royal dukes, Prince Charles attends the funeral of the Duke of Gloucester in 1974.

With a 'full set', Lieutenant The Prince of Wales, RN, signs the visitors' book at Barry during a four-day courtesy visit by his ship, the Bronington, in 1976.

32

Facing page: A fully qualified Royal Navy helicopter pilot, Prince Charles prepares for another take-off.

Left: The Prince, as Captain of HMS Bronington, *welcomes the Queen Mother and other members of the Royal Family aboard on his twenty-eighth birthday, Remembrance Day.*

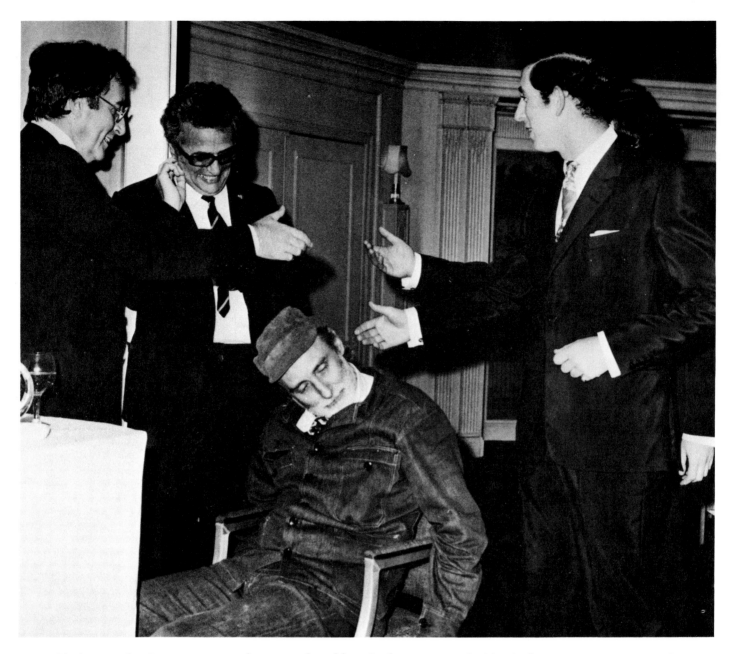

son assumed command, and later in the year, on Remembrance Day, the Queen visited the ship after attending the service at the Cenotaph.

Prince Charles had sailed home to the Pool of London in time for his twenty-eighth birthday, and this was to be his last in active service. In December 1976 he left the Navy in order to play his part in the Queen's Jubilee celebrations in 1977. He became Chairman of the Silver Jubilee Appeal, which he launched in a live broadcast from Chevening House. Its aim was to raise funds to be used for the benefit of young people, and within a year some £16 million had poured in.

For all the members of the Royal Family Jubilee Year meant a full and exacting programme and Prince Charles was no exception. In the spring there were visits to Kenya, Zaïre, Ghana and the Ivory Coast, and at home he found himself appearing on BBC

television in the programme *Nationwide* as part of the celebrations for the Jubilee. More honours came his way when he was appointed a Knight of the Thistle and promoted to Commander in the Royal Navy and Wing Commander in the Royal Air Force. He must have been reminded of the continuing problems of Northern Ireland when he was made Colonel-in-Chief of the Parachute Regiment for he had five years earlier attended a memorial service for the victims of an IRA bomb attack at their barracks in Aldershot, when he met relatives of those killed. Later visits to the regiment were to be much happier.

The climax of Jubilee Year came in June, and began with a reminder of an earlier Elizabethan Age. At Windsor Castle, with a special guard mounted by Members of the Sealed Knot in seventeenth-century dress, the Queen lit the first of a chain of bonfires, 102 in all, across the United Kingdom. In the days of

Left: Prince Charles sporting an HMS Bronington sweater with his own Prince of Wales emblem on the international ski trials course at Isola, near Nice.

Below: The Captain gives orders on HMS Bronington during exercises in the Firth of Forth.

the first Queen Elizabeth the bonfires had been lit to warn the people of the approaching Spanish Armada, but on this day, 6 June 1977, their message was more joyful and other bonfires were lit in faraway places such as New Zealand, unheard of by Queen Elizabeth II's famous forebear.

On Jubilee Day itself Prince Charles, as one of the Queen's personal ADCs, rode behind the Gold State Coach carrying his parents to St Paul's Cathedral for the special thanksgiving service. Although it was the Queen's day, few will forget the sight of her son's slight figure, in the scarlet uniform of a Colonel of the Welsh Guards, following the lumbering coach through the crowded streets of London to the cheers of the people lining the route.

In July 1977 Prince Charles paid another visit to Canada, this time to take part in centenary celebrations of a different kind with the Indian tribes in Alberta. He smoked the

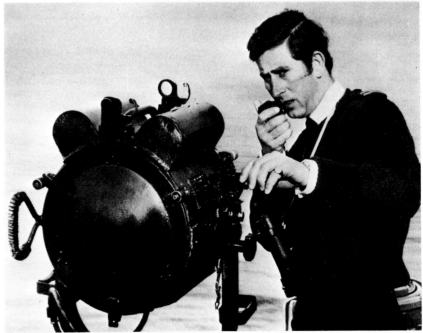

Right: The Royal Family on the balcony of Buckingham Palace after the Jubilee thanksgiving service in 1977.

Below: Prince Charles trying out a moon buggy at NASA in 1977.

customary peace pipe, unveiled a statue of the famous chief, Red Crow, and was installed as an honorary Kainai chieftain, the second white man to be so honoured. His great-uncle, the late Duke of Windsor, had been the first. Many ceremonies followed, during which the Prince's face was painted and he was required to put on the traditional eagle-feather head-dress. He was presented with numerous gifts, including a peace pipe, a handmade saddle and a horse named Cross Bell. Ever a participator, the Prince joined in the rhythmic dancing that rounded off the occasion.

Prince Charles's next engagement in Canada was at Calgary, where he was joined by Prince Andrew, who had also come to watch the famous Calgary Stampede. Both of them wore enormous white stetsons and string ties for the event, and Prince Charles led the stampede parade astride a black horse with a Western-type saddle, to the delight of the crowds.

In October the Prince went to the United States for a twelve-day stay during which he visited eleven cities. The strenuous pro-gramme afforded little time for relaxing, though he did fit in a game of polo at the ranch of the former US Ambassador to Britain, Anne Armstrong, as well as a small cattle round-up. The Space Center at Houston, Texas, was of great interest to him, and here he sat in a replica of a moon buggy. While in Texas, he also visited the historic Alamo, and had a slow river ride at San Antonio. Much publicity was given to his tour of Hollywood, and particularly to the beautiful film stars he met.

At the beginning of the following year Prince Charles took over the presidency of the International Council of the United World Colleges from Lord Mountbatten. The founder of Gordonstoun, Kurt Hahn, had been behind the establishment of the United World Colleges. Since he took on his new role

While attending a dinner in Belgrade in October 1978, during his first visit to a communist country, Prince Charles had the opportunity to talk to Yugoslav folk dancers.

37

the Prince has visited many countries to meet the students of UWC. In 1979 he flew round the world, visiting Singapore, Hong Kong, Australia and Canada and meeting UWC students in Singapore and Vancouver.

The Prince's thirtieth birthday in 1978 was celebrated in a completely novel fashion. After switching on the traditional Christmas lights in Regent Street in London's West End, he cut a huge cake in a clothes store. Earlier in the year he had been at an equally spectacular event, a dinner at Rio de Janeiro's town hall during an eight-day goodwill visit to Brazil in March. His meeting with an exotically clad dancer during a samba session provided photographers with a field day.

The year 1979 was a tragic one for the Royal Family. In May the Prince went to Lord Mountbatten's home, Broadlands, where his parents had spent part of their honeymoon in 1947, to perform its ceremonial opening to the public by cutting a ribbon. He was looking forward to the October wedding of Lord Mountbatten's grandson, Norton Knatchbull, to Penelope Eastwood, when he would be best man. The Prince was on a private fishing holiday in Iceland when, on August Bank Holiday, news came of the murder by the IRA of Lord Mountbatten and members of his family while they were on holiday at their Irish home, Classiebawn Castle. The Prince cut short his holiday and returned home immediately. With his father, he was present at Eastleigh when the coffins of the victims were flown home to England.

Prince Philip and Prince Charles both walked in the procession at Lord Mountbatten's State Funeral. It took place in London on 5 September and had been planned by the Earl himself. Prince Charles read the lesson from Psalm 107 at the service in Westminster Abbey. Members of the Royal Family, including Prince Charles, also attended the private burial at Romsey Abbey.

Top: Prince Charles and Prince Andrew 'suspended' on a parachute training course at RAF Brize Norton in 1978.

Above: With Balmoral in the background, a kilted Prince and his labrador, Harvey.

Right: Prince Charles, an expert shot, getting down to the intricacies of the rifle at Bisley in 1978.

In October, as his great-uncle would have wished, Prince Charles was best man to Norton Knatchbull, now Lord Romsey, at his marriage. He paid public tribute to Lord Romsey's grandfather again in December, speaking movingly of him and the other victims of the outrage at a memorial service held in St Paul's Cathedral. Prince Charles is today President of the Mountbatten Memorial Trust set up in the Earl's memory.

The Prince entered the 1980s on a sombre note, but it was an era that, in the event, was to bring him great personal happiness, as well as new challenges.

In July of 1980 it was announced that Prince Charles had purchased Highgrove House in the Cotswolds from the Macmillan Trust, and plans were afoot for his occupation in due course. It was noticed that the gates were somewhat shabby, with the result that one of his wedding presents was a specially designed new pair to grace the couple's future home. The Prince generously agreed that the old gates should be given to a charity in Bristol for use at a refuge home for women.

Prince Charles continued his travels in 1980, this time flying to the former British colony of Rhodesia, now Zimbabwe, to represent the Queen at the independence

On his thirtieth birthday the Prince switched on the Christmas lights in London's Regent Street, and is seen cutting a cake afterwards.

Above: Watched by the owner, his great-uncle Lord Mountbatten, Prince Charles opens Broadlands to the public for the first time.

Right: Representing the Queen at the independence celebrations in Zimbabwe in 1980, the Prince watches with Lord Soames as the Union Jack is lowered for the last time on the former colony of Rhodesia.

Escorting the Queen Mother after the thanksgiving service in St Paul's Cathedral for her eightieth birthday.

celebrations in April. He watched as the British flag was ceremoniously lowered for the final time, to the sound of the 'Last Post'. If the troubles in this part of the Commonwealth looked as if they might be over for a while at least, those in Northern Ireland continued and Prince Charles, as Colonel-in-Chief of the Gordon Highlanders, found himself visiting Armagh in Northern Ireland to inspect the regiment during its tour of duty in the province. His parents went to a less troublesome spot, paying their first State Visit to Switzerland in the spring to everyone's great delight.

The highlight of the year was undoubtedly the Queen Mother's eightieth birthday on 4 August. The celebrations came a little in advance in London, when, on 15 July, she drove to St Paul's Cathedral for a service of thanksgiving. Accompanying her in a state landau was Prince Charles. The Queen and other members of the Royal Family were also present at the service, including Prince Andrew who was by this time in the Royal Navy. In the evening the Queen Mother, again with members of her family (including opera-lover Prince Charles), was present at a special gala performance of *Rhapsody* at the

Right: 'The Patron' conducting a rehearsal at the Royal Opera House, Covent Garden.

Above: A royal author. The Prince of Wales's book for children is published in 1980.

Above right: The Colonel-in-Chief of Britain's Parachute Regiment meets India's parachute regiment during his visit to Fatehpur Sikri at the end of 1980.

Royal Opera House, Covent Garden.

Another happy event for the Prince was his emergence as a best-selling author. A children's story written by him eleven years earlier to entertain his younger brothers, Prince Andrew and Prince Edward, during a voyage in the Royal Yacht *Britannia* was illustrated by Sir Hugh Casson, President of the Royal Academy, and published as a book in 1980. Entitled *The Old Man of Lochnagar*, it is a charming story of Scotland, centred round a cave near Balmoral. The proceeds from the sales of this book go to the Prince of Wales's Charities Trust.

The year 1981 was to be a momentous one. It was heralded at the end of 1980 by a tour of

India, during which he met Mother Teresa, winner of the Nobel Peace Prize, at her Calcutta orphanage, giving her cases of drugs to help in her work. She gave the Prince a prayer for peace before he left to continue his tour, which included a visit to the Taj Mahal, where he was photographed in the traditionally romantic setting. He was a guest at the Presidential Palace in Delhi where his great-uncle, Lord Mountbatten, had lived as the last Viceroy of India, and while there managed to fit in a game of polo between the various official duties. During his trip he found continual reminders of the British Raj, not least when he visited the Indian Parachute Regiment at their depot and found the British

military tradition still flourishing in faraway Fatehpur Sikri.

Later the Prince flew on to Katmandu and he remained in Nepal for a week. Here he was able to relax and walk amidst the majestic scenery of the Himalayas. Of course he was given the traditional welcoming garlands of flowers and responded in true style and with his usual good humour.

His official visits over, the Prince relaxed on his annual skiing holiday in Switzerland. It was not long after his return to London that, to the delight of everyone, his engagement to the Lady Diana Spencer was announced, ending the years of speculation as to who his future bride would be.

Dubbed 'Action Man' by the media, the Prince of Wales has, by his general lifestyle and ready willingness to participate in any activity, however dangerous or unpleasant, truly earned this title. He seems never to be averse to 'having a go', whether it be performing daring deeds such as parachuting from aeroplanes or taking part in underwater trials, or even, as on an overseas tour, riding a child's bicycle round a park.

Prince Charles is good at a wide range of sports, from skiing to fishing (in the Scottish rivers, with his grandmother's encouragement). He is an excellent shot with a rifle and enjoys shooting at Sandringham and Blenheim and on the estates of the Duke of

Facing page: The Prince on
a bird-watching expedition
at Bharatpur during his
visit to India in 1980.

Above: Always energetic,
the Prince finds time to go
trotting after a polo match
in Fife.

Left: The Prince
acknowledging the
congratulations of supporters
of the Wynnstay Hunt at
Hanmer, near Whitchurch.
He had been staying at
nearby Cholmondeley
Castle in Cheshire after the
announcement of his
engagement.

*Right: Prince Charles
recovering after a 40-foot
(12·2m) dive to inspect the
wreck of the Tudor warship,
Mary Rose, lying off the
Portsmouth coast.*

*Below: Prince Charles clay-
pigeon shooting at Windsor.*

*Facing page: Wind-surfing
at Cowes in the Solent.*

Wellington in Spain. At game fairs he has even tried his hand with other weapons such as crossbows. As a naval man, he also likes sailing, usually taking part in Cowes Week. Other water sports are wind-surfing, water skiing and diving, even deep-sea diving when that proved necessary in order to see the wreck of the *Mary Rose*, flagship of Henry VIII's fleet.

Like the rest of his family he has a great love of horses and sports which involve them. He is famed as an international polo player, having been taught as a child by his father. Prince Philip gave up the sport because of injury in 1971 but, like Lord Mountbatten, retained his interest and passed on much advice to his son. The Prince is keen on foxhunting and goes out with the Duke of Beaufort in the Cotswolds and with the Belvoir during the season. He also competes in cross-country teams and has ridden in flat-racing and steeplechasing events. One of his horses, Allibar, died while training, but he rode another, Good Prospect, at Sandown and Cheltenham, unfortunately falling off on each ride and occasioning much amusement for the onlookers. On the flat, he was runner-up in the Mad Hatters' Prize Sweepstakes at Kempton Park on his horse Long Wharf.

A young man of many and varied interests, the Prince has another less-publicized but equally important side to his character. He is a patron of the Royal Opera House, Covent Garden, and has taken a keen interest in its work and in the Development Appeal launched in February 1979. His first official public engagement after the announcement of his betrothal to Lady Diana Spencer was to take her to a special evening recital of music, poetry and prose at the Goldsmiths' Hall, London, on 9 March. Also present was Her Serene Highness Princess Grace of Monaco, and this splendid occasion gave a real boost to the Appeal Fund, raising over £7000.

In June the Prince flew to New York in Concorde to attend a gala celebration of the Royal Ballet's fiftieth anniversary. It was his first visit to New York City, where he attended a performance of *The Sleeping Beauty* at the Metropolitan Opera House and was also present at a gala ball. Mrs Walter Annenberg, wife of the former US Ambassador to the Court of St James in London, played a prominent part in the proceedings, which raised money for three charities, the American Friends of Covent Garden, the Royal Ballet and the Metropolitan Opera Association.

The Prince shares with his wife a real love of music and is himself a keen musician, being an accomplished cellist. In addition to his liking for classical music, he also enjoys the

Right: Prince Charles, on Good Prospect, taking part in the Kim Muir Memorial Challenge Cup in the 1981 National Hunt Festival at Cheltenham. He was to fall at the tenth fence.

Below: A tricky moment demands all the polo-playing Prince's concentration and considerable skill.

Below right: A stern warning from a royal polo referee!

Facing page: A contemplative Prince with his gun dog, Harvey.

48

*Above: Prince Charles and
Lady Diana's first public
engagement together. They
are talking to Princess
Grace of Monaco at a
charity gala at Goldsmiths'
Hall, London.*

*Right: Making friends with
children in New Zealand
during the Prince's first long
separation from his fiancée.*

HRH the Colonel-in-Chief visits the Cheshire Regiment.

lighter kind with a distinct rhythm that sets his feet tapping. He appreciates the infectious humour and songs of the Goons, of whom he has been an ardent fan for years, and one or two of the stage appearances he made in his student days showed something of their influence.

Good as he is at interpreting the work of others, the Prince prefers to write his own speeches, which reflect his very positive attitude to life and his ability to take an interest in 'all sorts and conditions of men'. He has a wide circle of friends, many gained during Service life. Although he retired from active service in the Royal Navy in 1976 he still holds many Service appointments and frequently appears in uniform, in which he cuts quite a dashing figure.

Obviously this 'Prince Charming' has been the target for much speculation amongst the gossip columnists, and every pretty girl he has been seen in the company of has been marked by the media as a possible wife. One of those who attracted attention in Jubilee Year was Lady Sarah Spencer, elder sister of Lady Diana, who was in his skiing party at Klosters and watched him play polo. She is now married to Neil McCorquodale.

51

While visiting Christchurch in New Zealand in 1981 Prince Charles joined a lifeboat crew at sea.

Right: Another speech by HRH after receiving an honorary degree, this time from the University of Otago in Dunedin.

Far right: Naval talk. Prince Charles, Commander RN, with sailors of the New Zealand Navy.

Left: President Reagan and Prince Charles talk horses— and other matters—at the White House during the Prince's visit to the United States in 1981.

Below: Prince Charles making friends with the older generation during a walkabout.

Bottom: Eighteenth-century Highgrove House in Gloucestershire, country home of the Prince and Princess of Wales.

For some time Lady Diana Spencer had managed to stay out of the limelight, but as her friendship with the Heir to the Throne flourished the couple's meetings attracted more and more publicity. After the engagement had at last been officially announced and all the excitement had died down, the Prince had to undertake a long-planned five-week tour of Australia, New Zealand, Venezuela and the United States. He was seen off at the airport by a sad Lady Diana.

The people of Australia and the other countries welcomed the Prince warmly and there was much chaffing about his engagement, with some 'look-alike Lady Dianas' appearing in the press to tease him.

In the United States Prince Charles visited President Reagan at the White House, where he dined on saddle of lamb. The two men had much in common, especially their riding experience. While in Washington the Prince addressed an Oxford and Cambridge dinner, read the lesson at a service in the National Cathedral, and at the National Air and Space Museum revealed his considerable knowledge of aeronautics. At one of America's oldest cities, Williamsburg, Prince Charles received an honorary fellowship from the College of William and Mary, later touring the city and visiting the US aircraft carrier *Nimitz* at Norfolk.

After what must have seemed quite a long separation, the Prince returned home, to be welcomed at the airport by Lady Diana. The couple spent a short holiday at Balmoral before returning to London to prepare for their wedding.

Diana, Princess of Wales

Lady Diana Frances Spencer, youngest daughter of Earl Spencer of Althorp in Northamptonshire, was born at Park House, Norfolk, on 1 July 1961 and christened in Sandringham Church.

Her father, the eighth Earl Spencer, was born on 24 January 1924 and was a godson of Queen Mary and the Duke of Windsor. He was educated at Eton and Sandhurst, and during the Second World War he served in the Royal Scots Greys. In 1947 he became ADC to the Governor of South Australia, a post he held until 1950, when he was appointed an Equerry to King George VI.

During this time he was often a guest at Balmoral, where he enjoyed shooting with Prince Philip and other guests. After the King's death he became Equerry to his daughter and was acting Master of the Royal Household when he married the Hon. Frances Roche, daughter of Lord and Lady Fermoy, at Westminster Abbey on 1 June 1954. The Queen, the Queen Mother, Princess Margaret and Princess Alexandra were among those present at the wedding and it was one of the Society events of 1954. After the service there was a reception at St James's Palace for some seven hundred guests.

Besides Lady Diana, the couple had four other children—Lady Sarah, born in 1955, Lady Jane, born in 1957, John, who died in 1960, the year of his birth, and Charles, now Viscount Althorp, who was born in 1964, the same year as Prince Edward.

Unhappily, the marriage ended in 1969. Lady Diana's mother married Mr Peter Shand Kydd, with whom she now farms on the Isle of Seil in Argyllshire, and her father, then Lord Althorp, married the former Lady Dartmouth, daughter of Barbara Cartland, the romantic novelist.

For years the family lived at Park House in Norfolk, a stone's throw from Sandringham, and the Spencer children and the royal

Below right: Lady Diana with her parents at her christening in 1961.

Below: A first-birthday picture of Lady Diana, taken at Park House on the Sandringham estate.

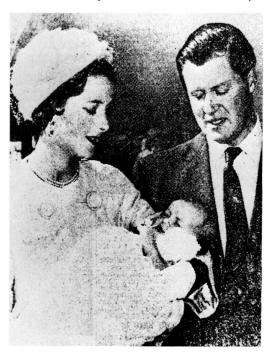

Lady Diana at Park House –
pram-pushing at a very
early age!

Earl Spencer (centre), then
Lord Althorp, walking in
the funeral procession of
King George VI at Windsor
in 1952.

Right: Lady Diana's father was in attendance on the Queen at a garden party held in the grounds of Government House, Hobart, during her 1953-54 Commonwealth Tour.

Below: Viscount Althorp with the Queen and Prince Philip in Australia. The Queen is walking with the Duke between a guard of honour of more than 350 Sydney clergy. Next to Lady Diana's father is Lady Pamela Mountbatten, Lady-in-Waiting to the Queen and daughter of Earl Mountbatten.

Below right: The Hon. Frances Roche, Lady Diana's mother, leaving with her father, Lord Fermoy, for her wedding at Westminster Abbey on 1 June 1954.

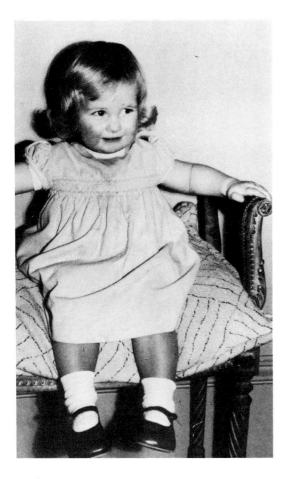

Far left: A charming study of Lady Diana at the age of two.

Left: Lady Diana giving her brother, Charles, a push. The photograph was taken in the summer of 1967 in the grounds of Park House, the Spencer home on the Sandringham estate.

children naturally grew up as great friends.

While Prince Charles can trace his descent from six earlier Princes of Wales, his wife's family tree is like that of the Queen Mother. Both have royal blood in their line, Henry VII being a common ancestor, and both are daughters of earls of ancient lineage. The new Princess descends from the male line of Sir Winston Churchill, and she and her husband both have a link with George Washington, the first President of the United States.

The royal marriage on 29 July made history in several ways. The last time a Prince of Wales married, as Prince of Wales, was in 1863 when Prince Albert Edward, son of Queen Victoria and later King Edward VII, married Princess Alexandra of Denmark. Lady Diana became the first Princess of Wales for more than seventy years, the last to hold the title having been Queen Mary.

When Lady Diana married Prince Charles it was the first time in over three hundred years that an heir to the throne of Great Britain had married a British subject. The last time was when James, Duke of York, brother to King Charles II and later King James II, married Lady Anne Hyde, daughter of the Earl of Clarendon, in 1659. The Spencers descend four times over from Charles II and once from James II, giving them six lines of descent from Mary, Queen of Scots. Prince Charles has no descent from the later royal Stuarts so Lady Diana reintroduces their blood into the Royal Family.

The Spencer family have a long record of friendship and service to the Royal Family. Almost five hundred years ago, when the Spencers were sheep farmers, one of Lady Diana's ancestors, John Spencer of Wormleighton in Warwickshire, bought Althorp in Northamptonshire, and was knighted by King Henry VIII. He claimed descent from William the Conqueror's Steward, Robert Despencer. His grandson, the second Sir John, married the eldest daughter of Sir Thomas Kytson of Suffolk, augmenting the family's fortune in the process.

Their son, the third Sir John, received his knighthood in 1588 and married the daughter of the judge who presided at the trial of the Duke of Norfolk when he was charged with high treason for conspiring with Mary, Queen of Scots, to take the throne of Elizabeth I.

Sir Robert Spencer (fifth of the family to be knighted) was Sheriff of Northamptonshire and a well-known sheep breeder. He was believed to be the wealthiest man in England at the time of James I. Created first Baron Spencer, he was the principal ambassador representing 'the Sovereign's person' at the investiture of Frederick, Duke of Württemberg, as a Knight of the Garter at Stuttgart Cathedral in 1601.

During the troubled seventeenth century Henry, second son of the second Baron Spencer, was created Earl of Sunderland in 1643. An ardent Royalist, he enlisted in the King's army on the outbreak of the Civil War and lent his sovereign £10000. In 1642 he was sent to Parliament as an envoy by Charles I, a year before he was killed at the Battle of Newbury. His son Robert, second Earl of Sunderland, became Secretary of State to Charles II in 1679 and afterwards supported James II before switching his allegiance to William of Orange. His second son, Charles, third Earl of Sunderland, held high office under Queen Anne and later George I, becoming Prime Minister in 1718. He married the daughter of the first Duke of Marlborough, with the eventual result that the fifth Earl of Sunderland became the third Duke of Marlborough, his younger brother succeeding to Althorp. The latter's son became the first Earl Spencer.

The two families of Churchill and Spencer divided, the former to take their place in military and political life, and the Spencers to follow artistic pursuits. Very rich, having

inherited a large sum from Sarah, Duchess of Marlborough, they became connoisseurs of the arts and were gradually able to build up the famous collection of art treasures.

The second Earl Spencer had a very distinguished career, becoming Lord Privy Seal, First Lord of the Admiralty at the time of Nelson's early naval successes, and finally Home Secretary from 1806 to 1807.

In the 1830s the third Earl, who was at one time Chancellor of the Exchequer and had a real love for farming, founded the Royal Agricultural Society of England and helped with the founding of the Royal Agricultural College at Cirencester, where Captain Mark Phillips was a student on leaving the Army.

The fifth Earl, twice Lord Lieutenant of Ireland and First Lord of the Admiralty from 1892 to 1895, was a close friend of the Prince of Wales. His half-brother, the sixth Earl, who was apparently rather a difficult man, served as Lord Chamberlain to Edward VII and George V.

The seventh Earl Spencer, Lady Diana's grandfather, was Lord Lieutenant of Northamptonshire from 1952 until 1967 and dedi-

cated much of his life to Althorp, taking great care to rearrange the picture collection and improve the house, which he opened to the public for the first time. His wife, Cynthia, was a Lady of the Bedchamber to the Queen Mother, who attended their Golden Wedding celebrations in London in 1969. The family seat received a royal visit when Queen Mary called there on her way to Badminton at the beginning of the Second World War.

Lady Cynthia Spencer died in 1972. Her sister, Lady Katharine Seymour, was a Woman of the Bedchamber to the Queen Mother from 1937 to 1960 and is now an Extra Woman of the Bedchamber. Both of Lady Diana's grandfather's sisters were Ladies-in-Waiting to the Queen Mother, who was bridesmaid to one of them, Lady Lavinia Spencer, on her marriage to Lord Annaly in 1919.

Lady Diana's family includes, in descent from Charles II and the Duchess of Cleveland, two Dukes of Grafton, a Marchioness of Hertford and an admiral. In the line of descent from Sir Winston Churchill, father of the first Duke of Marlborough, there is the fourth Duke of Bedford and the fifth Duke of Devonshire. From Lucy Walters and King Charles II there are four Earls of Lucan, and from the King and the Duchess of Portsmouth, five Dukes of Richmond, the sixth Duke of Bedford and four Dukes of Abercorn.

On her mother's side, Lady Diana's grandmother, Ruth, Lady Fermoy, is Lady-in-Waiting to the Queen Mother.

Top: The sixth Earl Spencer, Lady Diana's great-grandfather, photographed with his heir, Lord Althorp, in about 1910.

Above: The sixth Earl Spencer at the 1914 Garter ceremony at Windsor with Sir Edward Grey of Fallodon.

Right: The sixth Earl Spencer at a Pytchley Hunt meet in Althorp Park in 1914.

Left: The seventh Earl
Spencer at Althorp in 1923
with his daughter, Lady
Anne, and his sister, Lady
Margaret Spencer.

Below left: The seventh
Earl Spencer, Lady Diana's
grandfather, arriving for a
levée at St James's Palace
in 1922.

Below: The three daughters
of the sixth Earl Spencer –
Lady Adelaide, Lady
Lavinia and Lady Margaret
– outside Lavender Cottage
in Althorp Park in 1913.

The education of Lady Diana began at a preparatory school, Riddlesworth Hall at Diss in Norfolk, where she enjoyed sports, particularly swimming and riding.

In 1975 her father succeeded to the title of eighth Earl Spencer and the family moved into the ancestral home, Althorp in Northamptonshire. The house, which contains one of the finest private art collections in Europe, is surrounded by a 15000-acre estate and has been in the family for nearly five hundred years. The original building of red brick was erected by Sir John Spencer soon after 1508 and was surrounded by a moat. Over the years alterations have changed the size and shape of the rooms, and in 1786 Henry Holland was asked by the second Earl Spencer to remodel the house and grounds. The moat was filled in, and the gardens and park were improved with the help of Samuel Lapidge,

Below: Lady Diana's maternal grandparents, Lord and Lady Fermoy, pictured leaving a London wedding reception in 1933.

Right: The young Lady Diana, photographed while she was still a pupil at Riddlesworth Hall, her preparatory school.

chief assistant to Capability Brown. The present gardens, designed by W. M. Teulon, date from the 1860s, and contain, beyond the lake, a temple which came from the garden of Admiralty House in London and was bought for £3 by the fifth Earl Spencer, First Lord of the Admiralty.

There is much of interest in the house, including items that once belonged to the first Duke of Marlborough. There are some marble Roman figures rescued from the River Tiber and given to the Duke by his brother, as well as a red lacquer Chinese screen presented to him by Leopold I, Archduke of Austria, which he used on his military campaigns. The house also contains treasures which once belonged to Queen Marie Antoinette. Amongst the furniture is a set of mahogany chairs decorated with the family coat of arms but left without upholstery so that any unexpected visitors could sit on them in their outdoor clothing.

The art collection contains many paintings by Thomas Gainsborough and by Sir Joshua Reynolds, who in 1768 became the first President of the newly founded Royal Academy. The Picture Gallery, which is 115 feet

Above: The Pytchley Hunt meets at Althorp.

Left: A delightful engraving of Althorp in about 1835.

(35 m) long, contains portraits of each generation of the family since the time of Elizabeth I, when the gallery was used by the household and guests for walks on wet days. It has been the setting for banquets and presentations and was the scene of a glittering reception for King William III in 1695.

On leaving her preparatory school Lady Diana became a boarder at West Heath School near Sevenoaks in Kent. The school, which was founded in 1865, takes 130 boarders and a few day girls. Standing in its own 32 acres of grounds, it is well equipped for recreation as well as education. Queen Mary, the last Princess of Wales, was one of its pupils, so it already had royal connections when Lady Diana arrived. Her parents had been divorced before she went there, so she spent some holidays with her father at Althorp and others in Scotland at the home of her mother, who had by this time married Peter Shand Kydd.

After three years at West Heath, Lady Diana left at the age of sixteen to go to the Institut Alpin, a finishing school at Videmanette near Gstaad in Switzerland. During the time she was there her eldest sister, Lady Sarah, spent a holiday skiing at nearby Klosters with Prince Charles. It was Lady Sarah who, on a weekend shoot at her father's estate, reintroduced Prince Charles to her sister, then a sixteen-year-old, an incident to be recalled by the Prince in later years.

Lady Diana left her Swiss school in 1978. At that time her father, who had meanwhile remarried, was seriously ill after a massive brain haemorrhage. His wife, Raine, nursed him herself, and as he needed rest and quiet

Right: Summer 1968 and a little girl swings on the railings outside her mother's London home in Cadogan Place.

Far right: 'Who's for croquet?' Lady Diana wields her mallet during a game at Itchenor in Sussex in 1970.

The block of flats in South Kensington where Lady Diana lived with three girlfriends up until the time of her engagement.

Souffle, the Shetland pony, greeting Lady Diana at her mother's home in Scotland during the summer of 1974.

In pensive mood, Lady Diana on a visit to the Outer Hebrides in 1974.

and there was little Lady Diana could do to help, she went to live in a London flat bought by her father.

She shared her South Kensington home with three girlfriends, all of them working, and Lady Diana soon took a job herself. She became a teacher at the Young England Kindergarten in Pimlico and quickly endeared herself to her young pupils.

The tall, attractive fair-haired girl, who all this time was living a happy and carefree existence with people of her own age, was often to be seen shopping locally or at the exclusive Knightsbridge stores, or driving her small car to and from work.

None of her sisters had been debutantes, nor was Lady Diana. Lady Jane, the second of the Spencer daughters, was bridesmaid to Lady Katharine Worsley when she married the Duke of Kent in 1961, the year of Lady Diana's birth. In 1978 she married Robert Fellowes, Assistant Private Secretary to the Queen since 1977 and son of Sir William Fellowes, for many years the Sandringham Land Agent. Lady Diana was a bridesmaid.

Her eldest sister, Lady Sarah, is a goddaughter of the Queen Mother, and Lady Jane is a goddaughter of the Duke of Kent. Their brother, Viscount Althorp, youngest of the family, is a godson of the Queen.

In September 1980 Lady Diana stayed with the Royal Family at Balmoral, where she was helping her sister, Lady Jane, after the birth of her first baby. So the royal romance began.

Lady Diana's sister, Sarah, prepares to go sailing with Prince Edward at Cowes.

Back at her job in London, Lady Diana continued the daily round, seemingly impervious to the never-ending bevy of newsmen who dogged her every footstep. With a shy smile, she would fend off their questions as she got in and out of her car, now a new Mini Metro given to her by the Prince. Although she always managed to retain her composure, life was nevertheless becoming intolerable, and her mother wrote a letter to *The Times* asking if it was really necessary to harass her daughter in this way.

The Royal Family, attempting to take a quiet holiday at Sandringham in the New Year, were relentlessly pursued by reporters and photographers, to the fury of them all, and rumours began to circulate, especially when the Palace confirmed that Lady Diana had stayed there for three days.

It was at a dinner in his private sitting room at Buckingham Palace in February that Prince Charles finally proposed and was accepted. Very soon afterwards Lady Diana flew to Australia for a short holiday with her mother. The Prince telephoned Lord Spencer to ask for his daughter's hand and informed the Queen of his plans.

Above: Lady Diana shopping in London with some of her charges before her engagement.

Left: Lady Diana pictured with two of the pupils at the Pimlico kindergarten where she worked.

69

Right: The Earl and Countess Spencer outside Buckingham Palace on Engagement Day. With them is the Hon. Henry Legge, one of the Earl's stepsons.

Below: Lady Sarah, one of Lady Diana's two elder sisters, enjoying a game of polo at Windsor in 1977.

Facing page: The Earl and Countess Spencer in their London flat on the day the engagement was announced.

On Tuesday, 24 February 1981, Buckingham Palace released the news that the world had been waiting for. Prince Charles and Lady Diana were officially engaged.

After a private lunch with the Queen, the Prince and Lady Diana, wearing a striking blue suit and white blouse, posed for the eager photographers in the grounds of Buckingham Palace. Lady Diana, smiling happily, showed everyone her engagement ring, a large oval sapphire surrounded by fourteen diamonds in a gold setting.

Later, in the sitting room where he had proposed to her, the Prince and Lady Diana gave a television interview. The couple were obviously very much in love and very happy. No firm date had been fixed for the marriage, they said, but the end of July was a possibility, and no plans had been made for the honeymoon.

Lady Diana was very positive that the twelve-year age gap made no difference, and the Prince remarked that you were as old as you thought you were, and his wife would keep him young. As to where they would live, both agreed they wanted to be at Highgrove, the Prince's Cotswold home, as much as possible, where Lady Diana would help with the redecorations and renovations.

Smiling broadly, Lady Diana revealed that she had had no hesitation in accepting the Prince's proposal.

*Right: The Prince and
Lady Diana on holiday at
Balmoral, where Harvey,
the Prince's labrador,
demands all the attention.*

*Below: Highgrove, first
country home of the young
royal couple.*

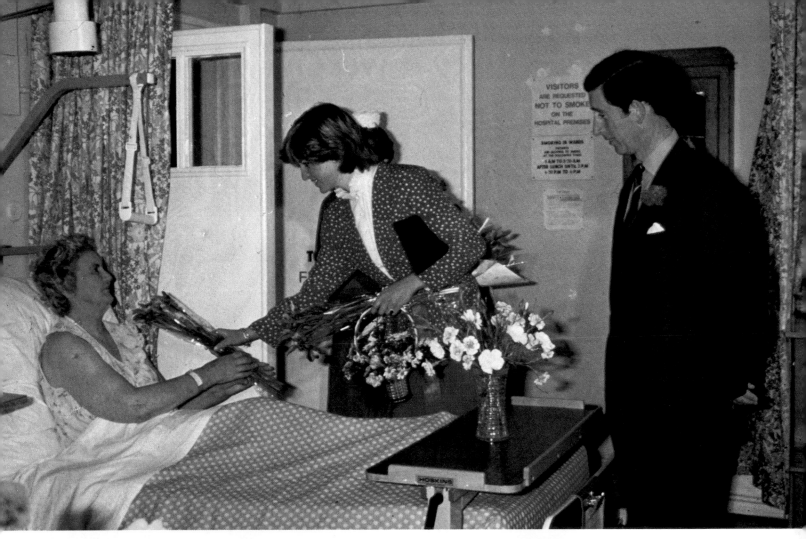

*Above: Lady Diana
distributing flowers, given
to her on a walkabout, to
hospital patients in Tetbury.*

*Left: Charlie Wright,
Balmoral's chief gamekeeper,
keeps a wary eye on Lady
Diana's attempts at casting
in the River Dee.*

Right: 'Getting down to it.' Lady Diana in earnest conversation with a small girl during her first public engagement with Prince Charles after his return from his overseas tour. They were visiting Broadlands, home of the late Lord Mountbatten.

Below: 'One for the album.' A charming smile from Lady Diana for a photographer at Broadlands.

Below right: A new life ahead, Lady Diana is seen leaving her London flat with her bodyguard after her engagement had been announced.

So, at last, Prince Charles had found the girl to share his life, and his fiancée was surely everything he could have wished for. Having grown up almost in the shadow of the Royal Family, she is at ease with them and welcomed by them. She shares the Prince's love for the arts, and for music in particular—her grandmother, Lady Fermoy, was a concert pianist and she herself plays the piano. Like the Prince, she is very fond of the outdoor life and of animals, and shared his sorrow at the death of his horse Allibar a few days before the engagement was announced.

She possesses a keen sense of humour and already brings to her task a youthful but slightly shy confidence that is refreshing and, at the same time, endearing. Tall and graceful, with silvery blonde hair cut in a casual style, she is happiest in simple, uncluttered clothes and wears the minimum of jewellery. She is not 'trendy', though, inevitably, she will set a style, and already her hairstyle and clothes have been copied by many girls.

As soon as the engagement was a fact Lady Diana was taken under the umbrella of pro-

tocol that hangs over someone of her rank. Her life changed completely on 24 February 1981, and would never be the same again. From sharing a Kensington flat with three girlfriends and taking her turn at washing-up, she went to live in royal palaces where there were servants to wait on her. No longer could she drive alone about London in her red Mini Metro; now she would be chauffeur-driven, with an armed escort at her side.

With her instinctive kindness, the Queen Mother invited her grandson's fiancée to stay at Clarence House after the engagement. There Lady Diana would have all the help and encouragement she needed, and would be able to call upon the knowledge and advice of one who had trodden a similar path before her. And there was the added bonus of having her own grandmother, Lady Fermoy, on hand.

Lady Diana confidently said on her engagement day that 'next to Prince Charles, I can't go wrong. He's there with me.' That confidence surely augurs well for her husband and for the nation.

Lady Diana starts to meet the people during a popular walkabout in Tetbury.

Princes of Wales

Prince Charles was created Prince of Wales on 26 July 1958, less than four months before his tenth birthday. While still a pupil at preparatory school he became the twenty-first prince since the fourteenth century to hold the title, an ancient and historic one which is much valued and not given as right to the eldest son of the Sovereign, only by discretion.

The first English Prince of Wales was Edward, son of Edward I, who had the title bestowed on him in 1301, and who, as Edward II, was to be foully murdered at Berkeley Castle in 1327. His hobbies are said to have included dice, theatricals, shoeing horses and thatching.

On through the troubled centuries other Princes of Wales have followed – first Edward, the Black Prince who won his spurs at the Battle of Crécy, later the Tudor Prince Arthur, whose father, Henry VII, realizing the importance of giving the Welsh people pride in his line, created his eldest son Prince of Wales in 1489, and on his marriage to Cather-

A portrait of the eleventh Prince of Wales painted by miniaturist Peter Oliver. The Prince, as Charles I, was to meet his death on the scaffold in 1649.

ine of Aragon sent the couple to Ludlow to receive homage from the Welsh nobles. When Arthur died prematurely in 1502, his younger brother Henry, later somewhat notorious as Henry VIII, inherited not only Arthur's wife but also his Welsh title, though this was not bestowed on him until 1503.

The ill-fated Stuart Princes of Wales were succeeded by the Hanoverians, the first of whom, George Augustus, son of George I, was said to have nursed a fanatical hatred of his father because of the way he treated his mother. He married Caroline of Anspach and the couple soon established their own circle, both setting out to charm the English. As George II, he was, at the Battle of Dettingen in 1743, the last British king to lead his armies on the field of battle.

Eighteenth-century Princes of Wales seem in general to have disliked their fathers, and the future George IV, better known as the Prince Regent, was in open conflict. As a young prince, he attracted the attentions of many ladies, whose company he loved, and showered his friends and acquaintances with lavish gifts. His lifestyle aroused bitter resentment among the people, not least because of his extravagance and wild living. He became the butt of cartoonists and his political enemies, and the culmination of their fury was soon centred on the Brighton Pavilion, which he created and filled with Chinese furniture. Fashion was important during his time, and such men as the Prince's friend Beau Brummell had many followers in the spas and resorts to which wealthy society people flocked in ever-increasing numbers.

Albert Edward, eldest son of Queen Victoria, was created Prince of Wales when he was twenty-five days old, and held the title until his mother died some fifty-nine years later and he succeeded to the throne. The longest-serving holder of the office, he spent many years in waiting, fulfilling his duties by

Above: The Black Prince, second English Prince of Wales, after his victory at the Battle of Crécy in 1346. The picture, by American artist Benjamin West, was painted more than four hundred years after the event and is in the royal collection.

Left: The fourteenth Prince of Wales became King George II in 1727 and as such was the last British monarch to lead his men into action. The artist John Wootton has pictured him at the Battle of Dettingen in 1743 when the French troops were defeated.

undertaking official tours abroad, and indulging his pleasures of country life when at home. Born in 1841, first male heir born to a reigning monarch since 1762, he was christened at St George's Chapel, Windsor. His many journeyings made him very popular abroad and he earned the name of 'Peacemaker' for his efforts to maintain good and friendly relations with his mother's enormous family of European monarchs.

In 1863 Prince Edward married Princess Alexandra of Denmark at St George's Chapel, Windsor. Queen Victoria, in mourning for Prince Albert, did not appear at the ceremony, which she watched from a gallery, dressed in black. The radiant and beautiful bride was dressed in a gown trimmed with myrtle and orange blossom and attended by eight brides-maids. The anthem 'God Bless the Prince of Wales' had been composed especially for the bridegroom in 1862. The honeymoon was spent at Osborne House on the Isle of Wight and the newly married couple took up residence at Marlborough House in London. This house, between the Mall and Pall Mall, was originally the home of John Churchill, first Duke of Marlborough, and his duchess, Sarah, was responsible for much of its decoration. These ancestors of today's Princess of Wales had another splendid stately home for they were given Blenheim Palace in Oxfordshire as a reward for the Duke's outstanding military service to his country.

Marlborough House was to become a home for queen dowagers as time passed, but for many years Prince Edward and Princess

Below right: A Cruickshank engraving of the Prince Regent. Son of George III and created seventeenth Prince of Wales in 1762, he was popularly known as 'Prinny'.

Above: 'The beauties of Brighton' in 1826, depicted against the background of the Royal Pavilion created by the Prince Regent.

Right: The christening of Prince Edward, eldest son of Queen Victoria, in 1841. He had already been created Prince of Wales.

Edward, eighteenth Prince of Wales, as a young man. Given the title in 1841, he held it for sixty years until he became King Edward VII.

Alexandra used it as their London home and it became the focus for London society. The Prince also acquired and developed one of the Royal Family's most popular homes, Sandringham House, in Norfolk, where he enjoyed the shooting which is still a popular winter pastime for the present Royal Family.

Queen Mary, wife of George V, was the last member of the Royal Family to live in Marlborough House, where she spent much of her widowhood. In 1959 the present Queen gave it to the Commonwealth as a conference centre, and it is now the venue for many important meetings.

Edward VII was a genial king who is said to have brought up his son and heir as a friend and to have reigned over his subjects as a boon

companion. In his time Britain saw many changes, not least the invasion of the roads by the motorcar, a means of transport of which he was an early pioneer. For her part, Queen Alexandra always took a particular interest in children and charity work, and not many years after her husband's death instigated the annual Alexandra Rose Day when flowers are sold to the public in aid of Britain's hospitals.

Their son became Prince of Wales in 1901, some months after his father had succeeded to the throne. With Princess Mary, whom he married in the Chapel Royal, St James's Palace, in 1893, he lived at Marlborough House until his own accession in 1910. The next year saw their eldest son, Edward,

Right: The wedding in 1863 of Princess Alexandra of Denmark and the Prince of Wales, the future Edward VII, as seen through the eyes of the Victorian painter, G. H. Thomas. The setting was St George's Chapel, Windsor, and Queen Victoria, still in mourning for Prince Albert, watched the ceremony from a secluded gallery.

Below: Along with his guests, King Edward VII poses for a group photograph after a lunch interval during a shoot at Sandringham. It was a favourite home, much used by him when he was Prince of Wales.

invested as Prince of Wales at Caernarvon Castle, the first to be publicly invested with the title since 1616. He became Edward VIII in 1936, but abdicated to marry a divorced American lady, Mrs Wallis Simpson, the same year.

Queen Mary, as Princess of Wales, was the last to equal Lady Diana in this rank, and though she only held the title for eight and a half years, her reign as queen to George V will long be remembered. With her tall, regal figure, she commanded love and respect throughout the world, not least for her dignity and courage over a long period during which she had to endure personal loss in the deaths of her husband and three of her sons, as well as watch Britain through two world wars.

Queen Mary played a very real role in public life, interesting herself in a number of charities, and in the Armed Services. She became Colonel-in-Chief of a selection of regiments, including the 13/18th Queen Mary's Own Hussars. The 13th Hussars was originally raised in 1697 and took part in a number of famous engagements, including the Peninsular War, the Charge of the Light Brigade and the Relief of Ladysmith. The 18th Hussars, with which it merged in 1922, took part in the Defence of Ladysmith, and both regiments fought with distinction in France during the First World War. The Women's Services were not neglected, the Queen being Colonel-in-Chief of the Women's Army Corps and the Army Nursing Corps.

A handsome souvenir of the wedding of a Prince of Wales in 1863.

81

Queen Alexandra meeting a
little Rose Day collector and
her dog, Yel, in 1923.

Left: The Duke of York and Princess May of Teck (later to be known more formally as Mary) with their bridesmaids after their wedding at the Chapel Royal, St James's Palace, in 1893. He was to become nineteenth Prince of Wales in 1901 and King George V in 1910.

Below left: The twentieth Prince of Wales in his investiture robes at Buckingham Palace in 1911. Prince Charles's immediate predecessor in the position, he was later to become King Edward VIII and then Duke of Windsor after his abdication.

Below: Prince Charles's great-grandparents, Prince and Princess of Wales for only eight and a half years, retained their popularity when they became King George V and Queen Mary, as can be seen from this rousing welcome given them in London's East End in 1922.

Right: Edward, Prince of Wales, is welcomed home from a tour of India in 1922. Beside him are his parents and his sister, behind them two of his brothers, the Dukes of Gloucester and York, and his brother-in-law, Lord Lascelles.

Facing page: To celebrate the 250th anniversary of the founding of the Most Honourable Order of the Bath, the Queen on 28 May 1975 installed the Prince of Wales as Great Master, the first time the eldest son of a sovereign has been made head of the Order.

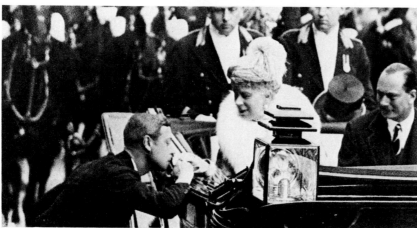

A greeting from Edward, Prince of Wales, for his mother, Queen Mary, as she arrives at Eton during the Jubilee Drive in 1935.

A knowledgeable and passionate collector of antiques, especially Chinese ones, Queen Mary was also an expert needlewoman, delighting in petit-point work. However, for those too young to remember the Queen herself, she is perhaps best known for her dolls' house, still on display at Windsor Castle. Designed by Sir Edwin Lutyens, it is a charming miniature country mansion, perfectly furnished in every detail and with paintings by famous artists of the day adorning the walls. The bookshelves have specially produced books by authors such as Kipling, Hardy and Conrad, some in their own hand, and there is even a Sherlock Holmes tale specially written by Conan Doyle. Everything works, including the lifts and the taps.

Unfortunately, Queen Mary died in March 1953, a few weeks before she would have celebrated her eighty-sixth birthday and her granddaughter's coronation in June. But the arrangements went ahead as planned by her special wish.

The Investiture of her great-grandson, Prince Charles, as Prince of Wales took place on 1 July 1969 at Caernarvon Castle in Wales, at a ceremony watched by millions on television. Afterwards, he was presented to the Welsh people by the Queen and began a tour of the Principality.

As Prince of Wales the Prince automatically became a Knight of the Order of the Garter. The Order, one of the oldest and most exclusive in the world, traditionally announces appointments on St George's Day, 23 April. The Prince was officially installed as a member of the Order in June 1968 at a ceremony in St George's Chapel, Windsor. Since then he has also become a member of the Crown's premier meritorious Order, having been installed as Great Master of the Order of the Bath at a ceremony in Westminster Abbey which took place in 1975 while the Prince was serving in the Royal Navy. As Great Master, he usually presides at the installation of Knights. The Prince is also a Knight of the Thistle, a Scottish Order founded in 1687 which fell into disuse and was revived by Queen Anne.

The Royal Family

And so to the Royal Family of which Lady Diana has just become a member.

Elizabeth Alexandra Mary, daughter of the Duke and Duchess of York, was born at her maternal grandparents' London home on 21 April 1926. No one imagined that one day she would be Queen of Great Britain. Her father was second in line of succession to the throne, and the young Princess lived quietly with her parents and younger sister, Margaret Rose. In 1936 her life changed. Her grandfather, King George V, died and was succeeded by his eldest son, Edward VIII, who abdicated only a few months later. The Duke of York unexpectedly found himself king, as George VI, and Princess Elizabeth became Heir to the Throne.

The King and Queen Elizabeth moved into Buckingham Palace with their family, and the young Princess began learning the difficult lessons of monarchy. She was educated privately, but extensively, concentrating particularly on history and languages. As part of

Princess Elizabeth accompanies her grandparents, King George V and Queen Mary, as they leave Crathie Church, near Balmoral, in 1935.

her education she visited many historic places and museums, and gradually became accustomed to attending official functions with her parents and grandmother. Soon after the outbreak of the Second World War in 1939 she and Princess Margaret were sent to Windsor Castle as a safety measure while her parents remained in London at Buckingham Palace, joining their children as often as their official duties would allow.

The young Princesses quickly adapted to wartime conditions, playing their part in the Girl Guides and knitting and gardening for victory in the grounds. On the lighter side, they enjoyed playing in the great corridors of the Castle, echoing and empty now as they were denuded of many of their treasures as a wartime precaution. Princess Elizabeth was able to increase her already considerable skill as a horsewoman, something she has retained over the years. Her interest was later to extend to racing and she is today recognized the world over as a very knowledgeable and successful racehorse owner. She prefers to race horses on the flat, while her mother is a successful owner of steeplechasers. The Queen has won many Classics, but so far the Derby has eluded her.

During the war Princess Elizabeth made her first broadcast, a message to the children of Britain, and at sixteen she became honorary Colonel-in-Chief of the Grenadier Guards, celebrating her birthday at a special parade in her honour. A few months before the end of the war she joined the ATS, the Auxiliary Territorial Service, as a junior subaltern at No. 1 Mechanical Transport Training Centre at Aldershot, where she proved a proficient motor mechanic and driver, though nowadays she drives only on her private estates.

After the war was over, Princess Elizabeth embarked with her parents and sister on a tour of South Africa, sailing in HMS *Vanguard*. It was during this visit that she celebrated her

Left : The balcony scene at Buckingham Palace after the coronation of King George VI and Queen Elizabeth on 14 May 1937.

Below : Princess Elizabeth and Princess Margaret with their corgi Jane on the lawn at Windsor Castle in 1941 during their wartime stay there.

Above: Princess Elizabeth and her sister 'knitting for victory' in the grounds of Royal Lodge, Windsor, in April 1940.

Right: Princess Elizabeth enjoying exercise in Windsor Great Park with her riding master.

King George VI and his elder daughter share a quiet moment at Windsor in 1942.

Her sister at her side, Princess Elizabeth makes her first radio broadcast in October 1940.

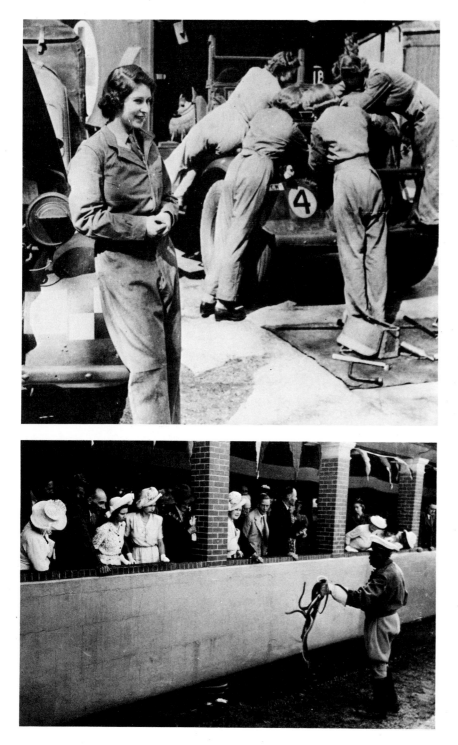

In 1952, while Princess Elizabeth and Prince Philip were on a tour of Kenya, staying at Treetops Hotel, King George VI died, and his daughter had to return home to take up the tasks of monarchy. She moved out of Clarence House, her home since her marriage, and back into Buckingham Palace, her mother and Princess Margaret taking her place at Clarence House.

Queen Elizabeth was crowned in Westminster Abbey on 2 June 1953. Throughout her reign her dedication and selflessness have been unchanging, and she has become something of a pioneer in her monarchy. She was the first queen to have had her coronation service televised and watched by millions all over the world. At the Trooping the Colour Parades she was the first to ride on horseback at the head of her troops since Elizabeth I who, four hundred years earlier at Tilbury, had exhorted her troops from horseback before they went out to face the Spanish Armada. Later queens preferred to ride in carriages when taking the salute at the Trooping the Colour ceremony in June each year.

In 1957 Elizabeth was the first British monarch to broadcast the royal Christmas Day message on television. Instituted by her grandfather, King George V, these broadcasts became an annual event and were a particular comfort in wartime.

The year 1969 saw a completely new and delightful departure, blowing away many of the cobwebs around the trappings of monarchy. The Queen gave permission for a royal documentary film, *Royal Family*, to be made and shown on television. The camera crews and technicians took up their places at Buckingham Palace and elsewhere, filming every aspect of the Royal Family at work and relaxing during a year. So the secret world of monarchy was revealed to millions, all the many preparations that precede state occasions, a banquet for example or a State Opening of Parliament. The behind-the-scenes planning was there for all to see and marvel at, for the organization of the Royal Household is incredible. The life and work of the Royal Family was shown, interspersed with little memorable personal moments, such as when the Queen, exasperated at a delay before a reception, clearly said 'Come on!' to her dilatory family! Or the moment when the young Prince Edward, intrigued by Prince Charles's cello, bent too close to look and was surprised when the string snapped and hit him on the nose, much to the amusement of his brother.

The Queen is the most travelled monarch in the modern world, undertaking long tours every year. The culmination of her reign so

Top: Princess Elizabeth during her training as a second subaltern in the ATS in the last year of the Second World War.

Above: The Royal Family visit a snake park at Port Elizabeth in 1947. It was during this South African tour that Princess Elizabeth celebrated her twenty-first birthday.

twenty-first birthday, and in an historic broadcast pledged her whole life to the service of the Commonwealth. In this she has never faltered nor weakened.

On the Princess's return to England her engagement to Lieutenant Philip Mountbatten, RN, was announced, and the wedding took place in Westminster Abbey on 20 November 1947. The bridegroom, who had earlier renounced his Greek title, was created Duke of Edinburgh on the eve of the ceremony. In 1948 the couple's first child, Prince Charles, was born, with the birth of Princess Anne following in 1950 and those of Princes Andrew and Edward in 1960 and 1964.

Left: The young Queen attends another religious ceremony. On her accession she automatically succeeded her father as head of the Church of England and plays a vital role in its life.

Below left: A wedding gift from the Girl Guides of Australia of the ingredients for the wedding cake of Princess Elizabeth in 1947. Post-war rationing made cake-making almost impossible in England at that time.

Below: The scene inside Westminster Abbey on 20 November 1947, the day of Princess Elizabeth's marriage to the Duke of Edinburgh.

far has undoubtedly been her Silver Jubilee in 1977 when the whole of the kingdom celebrated in a warmth of affection that rolled towards her like a tide. That year the Queen toured all parts of the Commonwealth, visiting countries as far afield as New Zealand, Australia and New Guinea, covering thousands of miles and travelling on about fifty separate plane journeys. At home, she celebrated with a special thanksgiving service in St Paul's Cathedral and was the guest of the City of London at a luncheon in her honour at the Guildhall. Everywhere she went children came out to present her with flowers,

Above: On honeymoon at Broadlands, Princess Elizabeth and the Duke of Edinburgh look through their wedding photographs.

Above right: Princess Elizabeth and the Duke of Edinburgh on honeymoon in 1947.

Right: An early picture of Prince Charles with his parents in the garden of their Surrey home at Windlesham Moor.

Above left: Princess Margaret looks on as the Queen Mother answers a question from her young grandson at the coronation of his mother on 2 June 1953.

Above: A family group after the christening of Princess Anne in 1950. Beside the baby and her mother are great-grandmother Queen Mary and grandmother Queen Elizabeth, who holds Prince Charles. Standing behind them are King George VI and the Duke of Edinburgh.

Left: A royal family group in the Throne Room of Buckingham Palace after Queen Elizabeth II's coronation.

Above: The Queen and the Duke of Edinburgh leave the Bermuda Parliament in 1953 during their Commonwealth Tour.

Right: In 1960 the Queen paid the first visit of a reigning monarch to the Shetland Islands since 1263. At Lerwick she opened the new harbour extension.

Bottom right: The Lord Mayor of London toasts the Queen and the Duke of Edinburgh at the Guildhall luncheon given to mark the Royal Silver Wedding Anniversary in November 1972.

sometimes a tiny posy, sometimes a bunch of cut flowers, and frequently a trembling, bemused child would be rewarded with a smile when a single, occasionally drooping bloom was offered. Her car became a veritable flowery chariot on all her journeys. These touching spontaneous gestures marked the desire of ordinary people to reach out and give her something in her special year.

The Queen is steadfast in her task and carries out her many duties with dedication and an interest which never flags. She quickly realized the need for a more expansive and friendly approach to her subjects at home and abroad and established the popular 'walkabouts' during which she and other members of her family are able to talk to many people in streets all over the world. Bravely the Queen walks freely through the crowds, stopping for a word here and there, always charming, receptive, but never losing one iota of her dignity or dispelling any of the aura that surrounds her. For all her slight stature, she has a commanding presence and there is a glowing strength which emanates from her. Throughout her reign she has been supported by the great love of her family and people which is a real strength to her.

Not the least part of the Queen's support comes of course from her husband, Prince Philip. The only son of Prince Andrew of Greece, he was born on the island of Corfu on 10 June 1921 and became a permanent exile while he was still a child. Philip, a great-great-grandchild of Queen Victoria, is descended on his father's side from a German ruling house and from the same Danish royal line (dating back to 1448) that produced Queen Alexandra, wife of Edward VII. His mother, Alice of Battenberg and Greece, was a sister of Lord Louis Mountbatten, whose family is one of the oldest traceable in Christendom, the House of Brabant. Lord Louis, one-time president of the Society of Genealogists in London, compiled a 'Mountbatten Lineage', a fascinating document showing how the family intertwines with the ruling houses of Europe, and a chronicle of European history in itself.

Prince Philip had four sisters, all older. His uncle, Alexander, succeeded to the Greek throne when his brother, King Constantine, was exiled, but in 1920 he was bitten by a pet monkey and died of blood poisoning. A plebiscite restored Constantine to the throne, but when Greece was defeated in the war with Turkey, he was again exiled. Prince Andrew was arrested, but later released, thanks to British intervention, and sent into exile with his wife, daughters and infant son, who had all been living on Corfu. The family stayed in England for a while, then settled in France,

The Queen and her younger sons relax over the family album.

The Queen looking at art work done by pupils at Benenden School when she visited it in the summer of 1968. Princess Anne, in her last term at the school, is second from the right.

Right: The Queen in
Kuwait in 1979 on her
historic tour of the Arabian
Gulf.

Below: Pope John welcomes
the Queen and Prince Philip
to the Vatican in October
1980.

and many European relatives helped them, in particular the family of Prince Philip's mother, the Mountbattens. It was Lord Louis Mountbatten's elder brother, George, the Marquess of Milford Haven, who was responsible for Philip's upbringing in England after he arrived at the age of nine. He was sent to a preparatory school at Cheam in Surrey, and holidays were spent with the Milford Havens or his parents in Paris. At twelve he was sent to Salem, in Germany, to the school run by Kurt Hahn, which transferred when the Nazis came to power to Gordonstoun in Scotland. Here Philip quickly made his mark and had a successful career.

The Marquess of Milford Haven died in 1938 and Prince Philip's father in 1944, so Lord Mountbatten rapidly became a great influence in his nephew's life. As uncle to Philip, he in some ways took the place of his father, and this influence was to manifest itself later when Prince Charles, lacking a grandfather after the death of George VI, turned to his 'unofficial grandfather' for counsel and friendship in the years ahead. It was perhaps inevitable, under the influence of Lord Mountbatten with his deep love of the sea, and with his own strong inclinations, that Prince Philip should enter the Royal Naval College at Dartmouth as a cadet in the spring of 1939. A few weeks later King George VI, with his wife and two daughters, paid a visit to the college where the King had

once been a cadet. Lord Mountbatten – or 'Uncle Dickie' as he was known to the family – was ADC to the King, and Prince Philip was selected as Captain's messenger. Thus came about the first meeting with Princess Elizabeth, which was to begin a friendship that later blossomed into love.

In the Second World War Prince Philip served with distinction and afterwards the long-awaited royal betrothal to Princess Elizabeth was official. After the wedding he continued his naval career, for a while going on to half pay as royal duties demanded more and more of his time. One of his offices was the presidency of the National Playing Fields Association, which he took over from Lord Mountbatten.

This was among the first of many appointments, for Prince Philip has been unstinting of his time and energy in a variety of fields, notably those of science and technology, where his enquiring mind is particularly stimulated. He became Colonel-in-Chief of a number of regiments and Colonel of the Welsh Guards (a position which later passed to Prince Charles), and he is Captain General of the Royal Marines. His interest in wildlife conservation, and in particular his support for the World Wildlife Fund, should not be forgotten. A keen horseman and expert polo player, he was forced to give up the sport after injury and turned instead to four-in-hand driving, at which he soon excelled. He is now

Above left: Prince Philip in Greek national costume in 1930.

Above: The night of the Duke of Edinburgh's naval stag party in November 1947.

97

Right: Prince Philip enjoying a game of polo in Windsor Great Park in 1956.

Below: A handshake between former brothers-in-law. Prince Philip greets Lord Snowdon at the Scottish Design Centre in Glasgow during a visit in June 1978.

President of the International Equestrian Federation, where his influence over the British decision to boycott the Moscow Olympics was noted, particularly as his daughter was a likely contender.

A keen all-round sportsman, Prince Philip enjoys cricket, sailing and active pursuits, his ever-enquiring mind ready to grasp new skills and interests, while at the same time enjoying the quieter pleasures of painting. He regularly undertakes overseas tours, sometimes at the side of the Queen, at other times on his own, and always his remarkable ability to put people at their ease is evidenced, his readiness to give a friendly smile or a word of encouragement.

Prince Philip has served the nation well, his contribution strong and sure, and has been more than just the husband of the Queen, for his humour has lightened many an occasion and his role has been carried out in a direct style conspicuously his own. Seemingly impervious to criticism, however undeserved, to all he seems approachable, the Royal with a glint of sympathy and understanding in his eye, not afraid to relax, nor hidebound by the trappings of monarchy. It can be said that the changes which have taken place over the last twenty-nine years since the Queen's accession are due, to a great extent, to the strength of character and lively mind of Prince Philip. His capacity for hard work, shared by the Queen, has given real inspiration and strength to all.

Princess Anne Elizabeth Alice Louise, the Queen's only daughter, was born at Clarence House on 15 August 1950 and, like her aunt, the Princess Margaret, was an individual from the beginning. Her mother succeeded to the throne when Princess Anne was under two years of age, and her new life at Buckingham

Above: Prince Philip displays his expertise at carriage driving.

Far left: The royal captain leads his team on to the field for a cricket match against Lord Porchester's XI in 1958.

Left: Princess Anne and her father crewing the yacht Yeoman XVI *in the Britannia Cup at Cowes in 1970.*

Right: Young Princess Anne's exploring hand finds a human obstacle in the grounds of Clarence House in 1951.

Below: Prince Charles and Princess Anne mastering the technique of xylophone playing.

Palace began. Her admiration for her elder brother led her to try and copy him at first, but her forceful personality soon led her to greater mischiefs. She early on displayed her passion for horses, and from the start was a fearless rider, taking many a tumble in the pursuit of her sport. Lessons in less boisterous activities such as dancing took place regularly at the Palace and a Brownie pack was formed there so that she could mix more with other children. In 1963 she was sent to a girls' boarding school in Kent, Benenden. Here she enjoyed sports, especially riding, and took part in a number of gymkhanas as a member of the school team.

On leaving school, Princess Anne dutifully performed her share of royal engagements whilst continuing to concentrate on her riding, and in 1971 she won the European Three-Day Event at Burghley. Princess Anne made many friends amongst those in that special part of the horse world in which she had chosen to compete, among them Captain Mark Phillips of Great Somerford in Wiltshire, an officer in the Queen's Dragoon Guards and an Olympic

In 1969 Princess Anne became the first lady to visit a North Sea drilling rig.

Princess Anne on her pony Jester competing in a pony show at Benenden in 1965.

gold-medallist. They married at Westminster Abbey on Prince Charles's birthday, 14 November 1973, and spent their honeymoon cruising in the Royal Yacht *Britannia*. Captain Phillips remained in the Army and was posted as an instructor to the Royal Military Academy Sandhurst, where the couple lived in Oak Grove House.

Captain Phillips has accompanied Princess Anne on a number of overseas tours, but the couple made their most sensational appearance in the world's headlines after the events of 20 March 1974. Returning to Buckingham Palace from a charity show that evening, they were attacked in the Mall by a gunman, who was trying to kidnap the Princess. After some firing and numerous struggles the attacker ran off but was brought down with a rugby tackle by a policeman. At his trial the gunman was found to be mentally deranged and was committed to a mental hospital. Several people were injured in the incident, but none seriously, and the bravery shown by those involved, who included several passers-by, was recognized when they were awarded honours by the Queen.

Princess Anne was appointed Chief Commandant of the Women's Royal Naval

Princess Anne, on Doublet, tackles a water obstacle on her way to becoming European Individual Three-Day-Event Champion in 1971.

Princess Anne and her fiancé, Captain Mark Phillips, at a charity film premiere shortly before their wedding.

She worked in her native Copenhagen and then as a secretary at the Danish Embassy in London before her marriage. The wedding was very quiet in comparison with other royal weddings, with no bridesmaids or pages. It took place in the thirteenth-century Norman church at Barnwell, the Northamptonshire village where the Gloucesters have their family home. The groom's elder brother, Prince William, was best man. In 1968 he had given up a diplomatic career to run the family estate when his father suffered a stroke.

Six weeks after the wedding, tragedy struck. Prince William was killed at the age of thirty, while piloting his Piper Cherokee plane in an air race near Wolverhampton. And so Prince Richard eventually became Duke of Gloucester, and as such has under-

taken many overseas tours and visits with the Duchess. His heir is Alexander, Earl of Ulster, who was born on 24 October 1974 and has two sisters, Lady Davina, born on 19 November 1977, and Lady Rose, born on 1 March 1980.

During the Second World War, Prince George, Duke of Kent and brother to King George VI, was killed in a flying accident in August 1942, while serving with the Royal Air Force. His widow, the beautiful Princess Marina, daughter of Prince Nicholas of Greece, was left to bring up their children alone, at Coppins, the family home at Iver in Buckinghamshire. There were two sons, Prince Edward, who succeeded his father as Duke of Kent, and Prince Michael, born seven weeks before his father was killed, as

The Duke and Duchess of Gloucester with their children after the christening of Lady Rose in 1980.

A tired Captain Mark Phillips at an early-morning equestrian event in Holland.

In 1977 Princess Anne, Chief Commandant of the Women's Royal Naval Service, attended a service in Westminster Abbey to mark the diamond jubilee of the Combined Women's Services. Pictured with her are Princess Alice, Duchess of Gloucester, Air Chief Commandant of the Women's Royal Air Force, and the Duchess of Kent, Controller Commandant of the Women's Royal Army Corps.

Overleaf: A wedding group photographed at Buckingham Palace after the marriage of Princess Anne and Captain Mark Phillips at Westminster Abbey on 14 November 1973.

Above: Princess Anne at the Chatsworth Horse Trials in 1977.

Above right: A quick word with a pony at the Open Day of the Riding for the Disabled Association in 1975.

Right: A competitor in the 1976 Montreal Olympics, Princess Anne is almost lost in a sea of hats!

Service on 1 July 1974, and she has played an active role, visiting many naval establishments and attending official functions. She is also keenly interested in the work of the Riding for the Disabled charity.

After four years of marriage, the couple's son, Peter Mark Andrew, was born on 15 November 1977 at St Mary's Hospital, Paddington, London, making the Queen a grandmother in her Silver Jubilee Year, and the Queen Mother a great-grandmother. Shortly afterwards Princess Anne and her husband moved into the Gloucestershire home given them by the Queen. At Gatcombe Park, with its large estate, they are able to farm and train their horses, Captain Phillips having taken a course at Cirencester Agricultural College on leaving the Army at the end of 1977.

On 15 May 1981 Princess Anne gave birth to a daughter, Zara, at St Mary's Hospital, London. Her last engagement before the birth had been to attend the wedding, at Great Somerford in Wiltshire, of her sister-in-law, Sarah Phillips, to Francis Staples. Master Peter Phillips acted as page boy to his aunt.

A family group after the christening of Peter Phillips, the Queen's first grandchild. Next to the Queen are her mother and Lord Louis Mountbatten, in front of whom is Princess Alice, Countess of Athlone and daughter of Queen Victoria's youngest son.

A proud wife and son watch Captain Mark Phillips competing in a riding event in Wiltshire in 1980.

Above: The Queen and her sons at the Montreal Olympic Games in 1976.

Right: Prince Andrew visits Prince Charles on board HMS Bronington *in 1976.*

Prince Andrew enjoying a game of rugger in Canada in 1977.

Prince Andrew Albert Christian Edward was born at Buckingham Palace on 19 February 1960, the second son and third child of Queen Elizabeth and Prince Philip, and his younger brother, Prince Edward Antony Richard Louis, was also born at Buckingham Palace, four years later, on 10 March 1964. The Queen's family was now complete, with a sixteen-year age gap between Prince Charles and Prince Edward.

From the outset, Prince Andrew was a very lively infant and the two boys enjoyed a happy childhood, though their education followed a slightly different pattern from that of Prince Charles. Instead of going to Cheam as their father and elder brother had done, Prince Andrew and Prince Edward were sent to Heatherdown in Berkshire, but both followed the family tradition by going on to Gordonstoun in Scotland.

In 1976 both Princes accompanied their parents to the Olympic Games in Montreal and Prince Andrew was a popular figure at the Olympic Village and at many events. They were able to see their sister, Princess Anne, competing in the equestrian events as part of the British team. Gradually, Prince Andrew took on more duties and was with his parents

Right: A twenty-first birthday picture of Prince Andrew at the controls of a helicopter.

Below: A salute for a proud, smiling father. Prince Andrew had just received his helicopter pilot's wings at Culdrose in April 1981.

Below right: Prince Edward and Lady Sarah Armstrong-Jones at Faslane, the Polaris submarine base on the Clyde, in 1974.

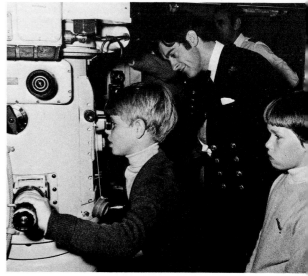

at many of the functions arranged for Silver Jubilee Year in 1977, even going to Northern Ireland, in spite of bomb threats, to visit the new University of Ulster. Just prior to this visit, the Prince had spent six months at Lakefield College School, near Peterborough, in Ontario, Canada. One of the highlights during his stay was a 208-mile canoe trip to the Arctic Northwest, sleeping under canvas. He returned to Gordonstoun to take his A-level examinations.

During the 1978 Easter holidays Prince Andrew joined Prince Charles on a parachute training course, and both were awarded their parachutist wings. Prince Andrew also took lessons in gliding at RAF Lossiemouth and qualified for his glider proficiency wings. In December 1978 he passed the selection test for training as a naval pilot and, like his father before him, opted for a naval career. He served at the Royal Naval College, Dartmouth, passing out at a parade taken by his father, who was delighted to present him with the coveted awards he had won by his own efforts. Now twenty-one, he is training as a helicopter pilot, and was one of Prince Charles's supporters at his marriage.

Prince Edward is still at Gordonstoun and was another supporter to his brother on 29 July.

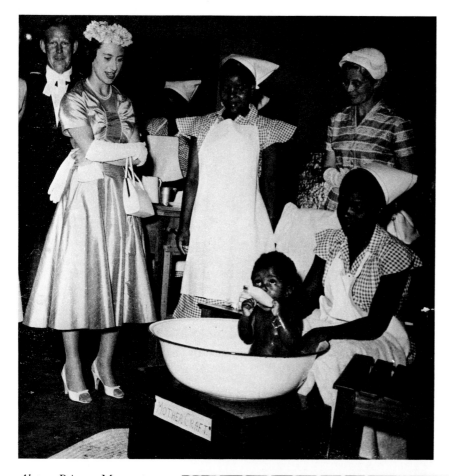

The Queen's sister, Princess Margaret, was born at Glamis Castle in Scotland, the home of her mother's family, on 21 August 1930, and from the early days the two sisters were very different, Princess Elizabeth more serious and dutiful, ever mindful of her calling, and her sister determinedly independent. After Princess Elizabeth's marriage, Princess Margaret was much alone and found herself thrown more and more into the company of Group Captain Peter Townsend, a Royal Equerry who had been chosen by King George VI. Unfortunately, he was a divorced man, some fifteen years her senior. He was at her side during her sadness at the death of her father, but in 1955 Princess Margaret bravely issued a statement that, 'mindful of the Church's teaching', she had decided not to marry Group Captain Townsend.

In May 1960 Princess Margaret married Antony Armstrong-Jones, later created Earl of Snowdon, at a ceremony in Westminster Abbey attended by the Queen and other members of the Royal Family, notably Princess Anne, who acted as bridesmaid. A well-known photographer and designer, who was responsible for the artistic setting at Caernarvon Castle when Prince Charles was

Above: Princess Margaret watching a mothercraft class during a visit to Tanganyika in 1954.

Right: Princess Margaret and Antony Armstrong-Jones with a canine friend at Royal Lodge, Windsor, before their marriage in 1960.

A dazzling patron of the arts, Princess Margaret arrives for another gala performance.

A word of congratulations from Princess Margaret at a St John's Ambulance Brigade Rally.

Above: An anxious moment for the Earl and Countess of Snowdon and their family at the Badminton Horse Trials.

Right: Princess Margaret and Lady Diana Spencer in the paddock at Sandown with Prince Charles before his unsuccessful ride in the Military Gold Cup.

Left: A royal admirer talks to ballet dancers Rudolf Nureyev and Sir Robert Helpmann.

Below: Prince William and Prince Richard of Gloucester having fun with their cousin, Prince Michael of Kent, at Battersea Fun Fair in 1953.

invested as Prince of Wales, Lord Snowdon has an inventive mind and has done much to help the disabled.

They had two children, a son, Viscount Linley, born on 3 November 1961, and a daughter, Lady Sarah Armstrong-Jones, born on 1 May 1964. She was the eldest bridesmaid at the wedding of Prince Charles.

In May 1978, eighteen years after their marriage, Princess Margaret and Lord Snowdon were divorced, and six months later he married Mrs Lucy Lindsay-Hogg.

Princess Margaret continues to live at Kensington Palace with her children and is known for her love of the arts. She takes particular interest in the theatre, films and ballet, and in 1968 was one of the party accompanying Prince Charles to Covent Garden to see Rudolf Nureyev's performance in *The Nutcracker*. The Princess enjoys other moments of off-duty relaxation during her winter holidays on the island of Mustique in the West Indies where she has had a villa built.

In 1980 Princess Margaret celebrated her fiftieth birthday with a party in London, at which one of the guests was Lady Diana Spencer. A great favourite of Prince Charles, his aunt is often seen in public with him, and with Lady Diana she was amongst those who

The future Duke and Duchess of Gloucester after their wedding at Barnwell in Northamptonshire on 8 July 1972.

Prince Charles and Princess Alexandra were two of the godparents at the christening of the Earl of Ulster, son of the Duke and Duchess of Gloucester, at Barnwell in 1975.

saw him thrown by his horse Good Prospect at the Sandown Races.

The Royal Family is a large one, and besides his aunt and cousins, Prince Charles has several second cousins, all of whom are happily married with their own growing children.

Prince Henry, Duke of Gloucester and brother of King George VI, died in 1974, to be succeeded by his architect son, Prince Richard, who was born at Northampton on 26 August 1944. He was educated at Eton and Magdalene College, Cambridge, and qualified as an architect. He is especially interested in art and photography, having illustrated a book, *On Public View*, in 1971, and others since then.

In 1972 he married Birgitte van Deurs, a Danish girl he had met while at Cambridge.

well as a daughter, Princess Alexandra. After her husband's death the Duchess continued to play an active part in the country's affairs. Having been appointed Commandant of the Women's Royal Naval Service in 1940, she continued in the office until her death in 1968. She took a keen interest in lawn tennis and was president of the All-England Lawn Tennis and Croquet Club, Wimbledon, being succeeded in this office by her eldest son.

Prince Edward, who was born on 9 October 1935, served in the Royal Scots Greys, and while stationed at Catterick in Yorkshire met Miss Katharine Worsley, daughter of the late Sir William Worsley of Hovingham Hall. In June 1961 they were married in York Minster, the first royal wedding there for more than six hundred years. They have three children, their heir, the Earl of St Andrews, who was born on 26 June 1962, Lady Helen Windsor, born on 28 April 1964, and Lord Nicholas Windsor, born on 25 July 1970. Lord Nicholas was a page at the wedding of Prince Charles and Lady Diana.

After twenty-one years' service in the Army, the Duke resigned with the rank of lieutenant-colonel in 1976 and took up the post of Vice-Chairman of the British Overseas Trade Board. He usually participates in Trooping the Colour, riding with Prince Charles and Prince Philip.

The Duke's brother, Prince Michael of Kent, was born on 4 July 1942, educated at Eton and Sandhurst and, like his brother, took up a military career, being commissioned into the 11th Hussars. One of his godparents was a close friend of the Kents, President Roosevelt of the United States, and the Prince was christened Michael George Charles Franklin in honour of his sponsor.

A lover of adventure, Prince Michael has driven a Formula 3 racing car round the Brands Hatch circuit in 65 seconds, been in the winning crew in a power-boat race and taken part in the Transatlantic Air Race. He was once injured in a four-man bobsleigh crash.

In 1978 Prince Michael renounced his right of succession to the throne—he was sixteenth in line at the time—in order to marry the Baroness Marie-Christine von Reibnitz, a Roman Catholic whose previous marriage had ended in divorce. The Queen gave her consent under the Royal Marriages Act, and Prince and Princess Michael (as she is now known) were married in Vienna in June 1978.

Below: The wedding of the Duke and Duchess of Kent at York Minster on 8 June 1961. Princess Anne and Lady Jane Spencer were among the bridesmaids. The last royal wedding at the Minster was when Edward III was married there in 1328.

Below right: Prince Michael of Kent and his bride, the former Baroness Marie-Christine von Reibnitz, after their marriage in Vienna in 1978.

Their son, Lord Frederick Windsor, was born on 6 April 1979 and their daughter, Lady Gabriela, on 23 April 1981.

Princess Alexandra of Kent was born on Christmas Day 1936, a fortnight after her uncle, Edward VIII, had signed the Instrument of Abdication, so she was born into a time of change and turmoil for the Royal Family. She was sent to boarding school at Heathfield in Berkshire and continued her education in France. On her return to England, she was quickly plunged into her share of royal duties and found herself representing the Queen at Nigeria's independence celebrations in 1960. Since then, this beautiful member of the Royal Family has carried out a great many engagements and her popularity is undoubtedly deserved.

In 1963 Princess Alexandra married the Hon. Angus Ogilvy, second son of the Earl of Airlie, at Westminster Abbey, with Princess Anne acting as chief bridesmaid. The couple live at Thatched House Lodge in Richmond Park, within the Greater London area, and have two children, James, born on 29 February 1964, and Marina, born on 31 July 1966. Their home was once occupied by a former Prime Minister, Sir Robert Walpole.

Above: A smiling Princess Alexandra after her marriage to the Hon. Angus Ogilvy at Westminster Abbey on 24 April 1963.

Left: Prince and Princess Michael of Kent with their son, Lord Frederick Windsor, after his christening in July 1979.

At Christmas the whole Royal Family traditionally gathers at Windsor Castle for the celebrations, presided over by the Queen and by her mother as 'head of the family'.

'My grandmother has been the most wonderful example of fun, laughter, warmth, infinite security and, above all else, exquisite taste in so many things . . . . She belongs to that priceless brand of human beings whose greatest gift is to enhance life for others through her own effervescent enthusiasm for life . . . . [She is] an inspiration and a figure of love and affection for young and old alike.'

So wrote Prince Charles about his grandmother, youngest but one of the ten children of the Earl and Countess of Strathmore, who was born at St Paul's Walden Bury in Hertfordshire on 4 August 1900 and christened Elizabeth Angela Marguerite Bowes-Lyon. Her mother, formerly Nina Cavendish-Bentinck, was a marvellous example of love, hard work, enthusiasm and artistic inspiration to her family.

At St Paul's the young Lady Elizabeth had a very happy childhood, with her younger brother David her constant playmate, and Bobs, the Shetland pony, a constant delight. She played at will in the woods and in the formal and informal gardens of the estate, and her very real and ever-growing love for flowers and country gardens was born.

Every year the Strathmores spent much time at their Scottish home, the mysterious turreted Glamis Castle. The Lyon family is one of Scotland's most distinguished and has lived at Glamis since 1372, the year Sir John Lyon was made Thane of Glamis by King Robert II. A future Chamberlain of Scotland, he was considered a fitting husband for the King's widowed daughter, Jean, and their marriage introduced the first royal blood into the line. Over three centuries earlier another Scottish king, Malcolm II, was said to have died in the royal hunting lodge which then occupied the Castle's site, though Shakespeare was probably mistaken when he placed the murder of King Duncan by Macbeth in 1040 in that setting. However, Mary, Queen of Scots, on her way to Huntly in 1562 to quell an uprising by the Gordons, definitely stayed at the Castle for her dinner menu on that occasion still exists. Over a century earlier Patrick, the first Lord Glamis, was associated with one of Mary's forebears in an unfortunate way for he was handed over to the English in 1424 as one of the hostages for King James I of Scotland's ransom.

Glamis is a unique heritage, reflecting more than a thousand years of history, beauty and service. The Castle, the church and the village are all living pieces of a great mosaic in which

The Queen Mother with some of her grandchildren and other members of the Royal Family after Morning Service at St George's Chapel, Windsor, on Christmas Day 1970.

120

figure kings and queens, saints, nobles, legends, wars, feuds, farmers and foresters, gamekeepers, stonemasons and crofters.

Lady Elizabeth was educated privately at home by a number of specialist teachers in an atmosphere of living history, for the Castle has many relics and treasures. The rooms which once echoed to the sounds of battle were now silent, but axes and armour combined with antlers to provide a reminder of their past. Amongst the family's treasured possessions was the watch left beside his bed at Glamis by Bonnie Prince Charlie as he fled from his English pursuers.

Lady Elizabeth was celebrating her fourteenth birthday when the First World War broke out and, after a visit to a London theatre, she heard the crowd at Buckingham Palace calling for their king. She spent most of the war at Glamis, where her life underwent many changes. Her brothers joined the Army, and one of them, Fergus, was killed in 1915 at the Battle of Loos. The Castle became a convalescent home for the wounded, with the Countess and her daughters helping to care for them. Lady Elizabeth fulfilled her part by helping the men to write letters, playing cards with them, providing entertainment on

Above: A delightful study of the Queen Mother, then the Lady Elizabeth Bowes-Lyon, in 1912.

Above right: Watched by her sister, Lady Rose Leveson Gower, Lady Elizabeth Bowes-Lyon shakes hands with one of the wounded soldiers who convalesced at Glamis Castle during the First World War.

Right: Lady Elizabeth Bowes-Lyon leaving her parents' home in Bruton Street for her wedding to the Duke of York at Westminster Abbey in 1923.

The Duke and Duchess of York on honeymoon in the grounds of Polesden Lacey in Surrey.

the piano and doing shopping in the village for them. They were her mother's guests and the Scottish tradition of hospitality was strong. She may even have been instrumental in keeping a roof over their heads for one night the Castle caught fire and it was Lady Elizabeth's prompt action in calling the fire brigades that probably saved her home from total destruction.

At eighteen, the war over, the young and beautiful Lady Elizabeth Bowes-Lyon came to London to take her place on the social scene. Through membership of the Girl Guides she became the friend of Princess Mary, daughter of George V, and was invited to Buckingham Palace where she met Prince Albert, Duke of York. The 'Sailor Prince', who had served in the Royal Navy during the war and seen action at the Battle of Jutland, was a friend of Lady Elizabeth's brothers and enjoyed visiting the Strathmore family at Glamis and St Paul's Walden Bury, where the romance between the Prince and Lady Elizabeth grew to fruition.

In 1923 the engagement was announced. It was a short one and the wedding took place at Westminster Abbey on 26 April that same year, the Duke's older brother acting as his groomsman. As she entered the Abbey on the arm of her father, Lady Elizabeth laid her bouquet of white roses and heather on the tomb of the Unknown Warrior, and when, twenty-four years later, her daughter married the Duke of Edinburgh in the same abbey, Princess Elizabeth's bouquet was laid in similar tribute.

After their marriage the Duke and Duchess of York lived simply and happily at White Lodge in Richmond Park, but it was at 17 Bruton Street, London home of the Duchess's parents, that their first child, Princess Elizabeth, was born in 1926. They had to leave her in Queen Mary's care almost immediately for in 1927 they were off on a six months' tour of Australia and New Zealand. The couple's

second child, Princess Margaret Rose, was born at Glamis in 1930.

In 1936 King George V died, to be succeeded by Edward VIII, who abdicated within the year in favour of his brother, the Duke of York. The lives of the Duke and Duchess were drastically changed. Prince Albert became George VI and the Duchess his queen consort, and with their young family they moved into Buckingham Palace to begin their arduous new life. At the age of thirty-six the former Lady Elizabeth Bowes-Lyon was wife to a king. Immediately, she began with her optimism and confidence to help her husband and her country, restoring family unity and enhancing the strength of the Throne itself. The reassurance provided by her smiling yet

The coronation of King George VI in Westminster Abbey in 1937.

Left: King George VI and Queen Elizabeth, accompanied by their daughters, inspecting Boy Scouts at Windsor Castle in 1938.

Below: The King and Queen leaving St George's Chapel, Windsor, after the Garter ceremony in 1937, their coronation year.

firm presence was to be an inspiration to her husband throughout all the years of their marriage. George VI was a good king in his own right; with her help he was a great one.

Queen Mary, the imposing Queen Mother, was there in the background with help and advice, but the running of Buckingham Palace was the new queen's responsibility. Gradually Queen Elizabeth established herself in the public eye, still serenely lovely, now more sure and confident, with her hands firmly on the reins. George VI appointed her a Lady of the Garter, a mark of public tribute, in 1936, and a Lady of the Thistle in 1937, the year of their coronation in Westminster Abbey.

The years passed and the King and Queen grew in stature and the respect they commanded. In 1938 a State Visit to France was greatly acclaimed, and a long-planned visit to Canada and the United States followed in 1939. This last visit, besides cementing friendships, made the King and Queen the first reigning sovereign and his consort to set foot on American soil.

The first year of the Second World War saw the two Princesses sent to comparative safety at Windsor Castle, while the King and Queen remained at Buckingham Palace. They worked tirelessly for the war effort, and their home soon became a shelter for royal refugees as the Nazis overran Europe. Queen Wilhelmina of the Netherlands, and Prince

125

Bernhardt and Princess Juliana, with their daughter, Princess Beatrix (now Queen of the Netherlands), were among the first arrivals. The Princess had not been christened, so the ceremony was performed in the chapel at Buckingham Palace, shortly before it was bombed. King Haakon of Norway was another guest.

The Palace was bombed nine times during the war and Cecil Beaton made a photographic record of the damage. The King and Queen paid many visits to bomb-damaged London, particularly the East End, and Queen Elizabeth was said to have remarked that, now her own home had been damaged, she felt she could 'look the East End in the face'. The royal travellers also visited many other parts of the kingdom to see troops, factories and other places, journeying some half a million miles in the royal train. Always the Queen's knack of making everyone feel better did immense good.

The war over, things gradually returned to normality. In 1947 Princess Elizabeth married, and in April 1948 the King and Queen celebrated their Silver Wedding with a thanksgiving service in St Paul's Cathedral. Later that year, on 14 November, there was great rejoicing when Princess Elizabeth gave birth to her first son, Prince Charles. The joy was marred by the increasing ill-health of the King, who early in 1949, encouraged by his indefatigable wife, successfully underwent

surgery. In 1950 Princess Anne was born, and the King and Queen had two young grandchildren from whom they derived much pleasure.

On 31 January 1952 Princess Elizabeth and the Duke of Edinburgh, deputizing for the King, set out on a planned five months' tour of Australia and New Zealand. They had got no further than Kenya when, on 6 February, the King was found dead in his bed by his valet at Sandringham. His daughter, now Queen, had to return to London immediately to take up her new duties, and his widow, now Queen Mother, had to face the terrible prospect of life without her husband. 'That most valiant woman', as Sir Winston Churchill once described her, was not lacking in the courage and fortitude necessary to begin her new role, supporting her young daughter and family and continuing to play her part in public life.

Immediately after the King's death Queen Elizabeth moved into Clarence House, and in May she undertook her first public engagement as Queen Mother, journeying to Scotland to inspect the First Battalion of the Black Watch, of which she had been Colonel-in-Chief since 1937, before they left for service in Korea. This was a special regiment to her–it was her 'family' regiment, and in its service her brother Fergus had been killed in France in 1915. Other servicemen were remembered when she unveiled the Commando Memorial at Spean Bridge shortly afterwards. She had emerged into the world again, resolutely putting personal feelings aside and taking up her new role.

At about this time the Queen Mother bought herself a castle in Scotland–the sixteenth-century sandstone Barrogill Castle, sitting like a fortress on the coastline of the Pentland Firth a few miles from Thurso. The Castle was old and worn, but the Queen Mother gave it new life, restoring it carefully, planning the rooms and gardens and giving it back its original name, the Castle of Mey. Every summer she spends a holiday there in her own special haven.

Mey is almost at the most northerly point of the British mainland and from the back windows of the Castle one can see across the Pentland Firth to the cliffs of Stroma and beyond them the grey-green of the Orkney Islands amidst the ever-moving sea. Grey geese flown in from the Arctic wastes march with their peculiar dignity over the green fields where sturdy black Aberdeen Angus cattle graze with impervious calm.

A miniature castle, once the home of the Earls of Caithness and set in country long ago ravaged by the Vikings, Mey is a fine home for a Lyon of Glamis.

The Queen Mother is a lady of many interests, being president or patron of over three hundred organizations, including the Royal Academy of Music, the Girl Guides, the Women's Section of the Royal British Legion, the Women's Royal Voluntary Service and the Young Women's Christian Association. She is Colonel-in-Chief of a

The Queen Mother, assisted by her daughter and grandchildren, helps out at a sale of work at Abergeldie Castle. It was organized by her in aid of funds for Crathie Church, where the Royal Family worship when at Balmoral.

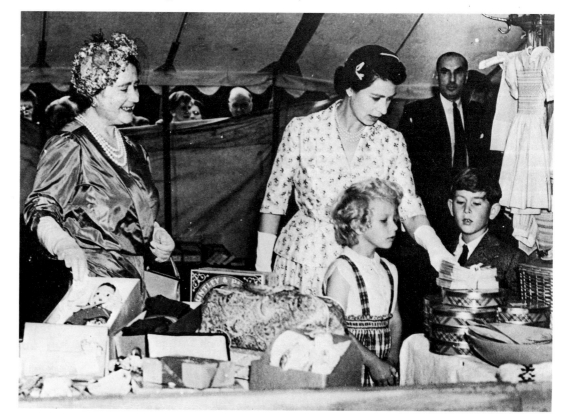

Above: After the 1980 Royal Variety Performance, given in her honour, the Queen Mother has a word with one of the artistes, Mary Martin, whose son, Larry Hagman ('JR'), looks on. Also watching are Bruce Forsyth and Cleo Laine.

Left: The Queen Mother talks to her great-nephew, Lord Glamis, at a passing-out parade at the Royal Military Academy Sandhurst in March 1981.

Above: The Queen Mother has a special pat for her corgi as she poses for a family photograph after the thanksgiving service for her eightieth birthday in 1980.

Right: Many happy returns! The Queen Mother on her seventieth birthday with three of her grandchildren, Prince Edward, Viscount Linley and Lady Sarah Armstrong-Jones.

number of regiments and Commandant-in-Chief of all three British women's services. She is Chancellor of many universities in Britain and the Commonwealth, and in 1954 she was made Master of the Bench of the Middle Temple in London. Over the years she has made many tours, and in 1958 was the first member of the Royal Family to fly round the world. She performs every duty at home or abroad as if it were for the first time, bringing with her that precious gift of spontaneity that is so much admired.

In 1979 the Queen Mother received a singular honour – her appointment as the first woman to hold the office of Lord Warden and Admiral of the Cinque Ports. But 1980 was a very special year, when she celebrated her eightieth birthday, an event shared, so it seemed, by the whole nation! It culminated in a service of thanksgiving at St Paul's Cathedral at which she had the special honour of taking precedence over the Queen, and where the nation acknowledged its true good fortune in having a Queen Mother who is admired and

loved by all who come into contact with her. Whatever the occasion, she adds grace and charm to it by her very presence.

On the private side, the Queen Mother has been a devoted wife, mother and grand-mother, the confidante and friend of all. Beloved by her family, she is its fountain and its source, enriching the fabric of its life at every turn.

The Queen Mother has a true love of animals, particularly dogs and horses. It was as Duchess of York that she introduced the Royal Family to the delightful Welsh corgi breed by giving her young daughter, Princess Elizabeth, a Pembrokeshire corgi puppy. Since that day in 1933 the Royal Family have had a succession of corgis as well as dogs of other breeds, many of whom are buried in the grounds where their mistress spent hours walking with them. A real outdoor person, she has never been deterred from her exercise by the weather.

The Queen Mother is an expert fisher-woman, especially of Scottish salmon, and has taught Prince Charles and Prince Edward some of her skills. But she is perhaps best known on the sporting scene as one of the most successful National Hunt owners. By gracing its meetings with her presence she has also played a strong part in the emerging popularity of the sport. For a long time she has ruled supreme as First Lady of 'Chasing' and is admired by owners, trainers, jockeys and lads alike, who respect and love her for her obvious enjoyment of the sport and for her professional eye.

The Queen Mother enjoys all forms of horseracing, but concentrates particularly on steeplechasing. Perhaps her most famous horse was Devon Loch, which ran in the 1956 Grand National at Aintree. The horse, winning post in sight, was fifteen lengths ahead of its nearest challenger when it collapsed and was passed by the rest of the field, in front of its royal owner. She took defeat philosophically, being more concerned about the feelings of Dick Francis, her jockey. The horse ended its days happily on the green pastures of Sandringham.

The Queen Mother regularly attends the Three-Day Badminton Horse Trials and the National Hunt Festival at Cheltenham. Lady Diana quickly found herself caught up in this royal obsession with horses, for one of her first public engagements after her betrothal was announced was to attend the Grand

Military Meeting at Sandown in the company of the Queen Mother and Princess Margaret. There they saw Prince Charles taking part in the Military Gold Cup on his horse Good Prospect.

No one disputes that the Queen Mother, with her charm and energy, is able to transform the everyday lives of those with whom she comes into contact. She even gives a new life to the houses she lives in, whether they are old castles in Scotland or houses in London or Windsor. Truly she is a living example of those who, as Kipling said, can 'walk with kings–nor lose the common touch'.

It was very appropriate that Prince Charles, her special first grandchild, should have given his fiancée into the Queen Mother's keeping before he took on the responsibility himself. Surely no one was more fitted to the task of helping Lady Diana than the Queen Mother. As the daughter of an earl herself and as one who has also had to adapt to the strictures of court life, who better to help the girl chosen by the Prince of Wales to stand at his side in the future?

When the Queen Mother was widowed in 1952 Prince Charles lost a grandfather, and at a very early age. Fortunately there was in the Royal Family a man, beloved of all and known as 'Uncle Dickie', who had already had a part in caring for the fatherless Prince Philip. He soon became an unofficial grand-

Lord Mountbatten and the former Edwina Ashley leave St Margaret's, Westminster, under a naval guard of honour after their marriage in July 1922.

Left: In 1950 Princess Elizabeth acted as godmother to the second son of Lord and Lady Brabourne, son-in-law and eldest daughter of Lord and Lady Mountbatten.

Below: On a rocky outcrop in Malta in 1954 the young Prince Charles enjoys a game with his great-uncle, Lord Mountbatten.

father to the young prince, and a friendship developed that was to last all the older man's life.

Born a few weeks before the Queen Mother, Admiral Lord Louis Mountbatten was a great-grandson of Queen Victoria, who asked that he be called Albert after her dear husband and held him in her arms during his christening. From the outset, Louis Mountbatten had a clear destiny. He followed his father, Prince Louis of Battenberg, into service with the Royal Navy, in which he had a distinguished career, culminating in the achievement in 1955 of his ambition to equal his father as First Sea Lord.

As a young naval officer he married Edwina Ashley at St Margaret's, Westminster, in 1922, with his great friend, Prince Edward, Prince of Wales, as best man. The couple had two daughters, the eldest of whom, Patricia,

Lord Louis Mountbatten, Supreme Allied Commander, South-East Asia, accepts the Japanese surrender in 1945.

succeeded to the Mountbatten title as Countess, whilst the other, Pamela, became the wife of the well-known interior designer, David Hicks.

Lord Mountbatten's career was remarkable by any standards. During the war he was Head of Combined Operations, playing his part in the planning of the D-Day landings in 1944. Later he was Supreme Commander in South-East Asia, receiving the Japanese surrender at Singapore in 1945. In 1947 he became the last Viceroy of India during the change-over to independence, and from 1947 until 1948 was Governor-General. Afterwards he was created the first Earl Mountbatten of Burma. In 1953 he was appointed personal ADC to the Queen and in 1956 Admiral of the Fleet. From 1965, in his role as Colonel of the Life Guards, he fulfilled his duties as Gold Stick in Waiting and participated in Trooping the Colour ceremonies as escort to the Sovereign. He was Colonel Commandant of the Royal Marines and a Governor of the Isle of Wight, and in 1946 he became a Knight of the Garter as well as first Freeman of Romsey in Hampshire, where his home, Broadlands, was the honeymoon venue for Princess Elizabeth and the Duke of Edinburgh in 1947.

There was always a special relationship between Lord Louis and Prince Charles, who spent many happy hours in his company

Left: The last Viceroy and Vicereine of India with some of their aides at the Viceroy's house in New Delhi.

Below: Princess Anne had her binoculars trained out to sea when she and her parents joined Lord Mountbatten at a NATO Review.

during his time at Cambridge and in the Royal Navy. They had many things in common, not least a great love of their country and of the game of polo, in which both of them excelled.

When Lord Louis was brutally murdered by the IRA on 27 August 1979 while at the helm of his boat, *Shadow V*, during a holiday at his Irish home, the Royal Family, and Prince Charles in particular, lost a very real friend. The Admiral was given his due, the State Funeral he had himself planned, with Prince Philip and Prince Charles walking in the procession. The Queen and many other members of the Royal Family attended the service, at which Prince Charles read the lesson. Lord Louis's body was later buried at

Romsey Abbey at a private service attended by the Royal Family. In December 1979, at a memorial service in St Paul's Cathedral, Prince Charles delivered a moving address, speaking of the 'mindless cruelty' of the murderers who had robbed his family of a great friend and his country of a great man.

In May 1981, shortly after Prince Charles's return from a five-week overseas tour, he and Lady Diana went to Lord Mountbatten's home at Broadlands, where the Prince opened an exhibition in his memory. Afterwards both walked about the grounds, talking to the many who had come to see them, and Lady Diana, in her first 'walkabout', picked up a baby held out to her, to the delight of the photographers.

A Royal Year

The royal year follows a well-established pattern, governed largely by rigid tradition. The pattern may vary to accommodate state tours and visits, but in normal times January sees the Royal Family at Sandringham House in Norfolk after the Christmas festivities.

Sandringham, the private property of the Queen, came into royal possession in 1861 when Queen Victoria and Prince Albert purchased the estate from the revenues of the Duchy of Cornwall for their eldest son, the Prince of Wales, later Edward VII. He loved the house, as succeeding generations have loved it. He remodelled it, adding a bowling alley and billiards and smoking rooms. Then he took it all down and started again, creating the present house.

The large estate provides excellent shooting which is much enjoyed by Prince Philip and Prince Charles. The royal studs are at Sandringham and also at nearby Wolferton, and here the Queen's racehorses, event horses (she bred Doublet, the horse on which Princess Anne won the European Championship), carriage horses, polo and other ponies are bred. Royal show dogs, introduced by George V, and labradors and corgis are in the kennels, and the whole atmosphere is one of relaxation. There are even royal pigeons. An innovation of George V, the birds saw active service in the Second World War.

The Queen and her mother belong to the local branch of the Women's Institute and the family attend Sunday services in the small church. Sandringham has been a family home for generations, loved by George V, who made his first Christmas radio broadcast from there, and by George VI, who died there and whose body, before being taken to London for the funeral, lay in state in the Sandringham church, guarded by workers from the estate. It was from Sandringham that his daughter made her first televised Christmas broadcast.

The amount of farming done on the estate has increased during the present Queen's reign, and produce from the estate not used at Buckingham Palace is sold to the public. In Jubilee Year a museum was opened in buildings formerly the coach house, fire station and power house, and the proceeds from this go to charity and towards upkeep of the house and gardens.

The brief holiday over, the Queen returns to her official London residence, Buckingham Palace. This famous royal home was originally built in 1702 by the Duke of Buckingham and named after him. George III bought it, renamed it 'Queen's House' in honour of his wife, and used the place as a family home.

A view of the Saloon at Sandringham House, showing one of the fine tapestries. The house was opened to the public for the first time in May 1977.

*Above: A view of
Sandringham House from
across the Upper Lake. A
favourite royal home since
Queen Victoria's days, it is
the private property of the
monarch.*

*Left: Alexandra, Princess of
Wales, in the garden at
Sandringham with her dogs
in 1900.*

139

A tranquil day in July 1893. The Duke of York, the future King George V, sails his canoe across the lake at York Cottage in the grounds of Sandringham.

King George V and Queen Mary with their daughter, Princess Mary, in the garden at Buckingham Palace in May 1915.

George IV decided to enlarge the house with the help of architect John Nash, but after nine years the work was still not finished and the King died before he could move in. His brother, William IV, had the building completed under another architect, but never lived there. The first sovereign to make it the seat of monarchy was Queen Victoria, who took up residence on the twenty-fourth day of her reign. The Palace was redesigned, a fourth wing was added, and the Marble Arch, designed by Nash to grace the main entrance, was removed to Hyde Park, where it remains to this day. The name of the first owner was perpetuated when the Palace was renamed after him.

Nowadays the Palace is the largest functioning one in the world, with over two hundred people employed inside, moving along the one and a half miles of corridor. Some of their titles go back centuries. There is the Master of the Household, who has overall responsibility for many departments, while the Lord Chamberlain takes overall responsibility for the whole. The latter's title originated in Norman times and long ago he was the only person to hold the key to the King's bedroom and his money. These days garden parties and state visits are more his concern.

Buckingham Palace has been described as 'almost a village', having its own police and fire stations and its own telephone exchange and post office. There is a filling station there, and a smithy and maintenance workshops, as well as a sick bay and a shop.

The general public see the East Front facing the Mall and the Victoria Memorial, and it is the focal point on many royal occasions. To the cheers of thousands the Queen and her immediate predecessors have appeared there with their families to wave after coronations, weddings, jubilees and other events. The new balcony was first used in 1854 by Queen Victoria when she watched the last Guards battalion march out of the courtyard before embarking for the Crimea.

King George VI and Queen Elizabeth walk through the ploughed-up grounds of Sandringham with their daughters. The year was 1943 and the Royal Family were making their contribution to wartime food production.

Right: The Music Room at
Buckingham Palace.
Designed by John Nash, it
overlooks forty acres of
gardens and has been the
scene of many royal
christenings, including that
of Prince Charles.

Below: The East Front of
Buckingham Palace in 1827,
as it appears in an engraving
made from a drawing by
Pugin.

*Above: The Queen and
Prince Philip outside
Worcester Cathedral after
the Royal Maundy Service
in 1980.*

*Left: The grounds of
Buckingham Palace are the
setting for many garden
parties. Here Princess
Elizabeth is seen talking to
guests in 1951.*

143

Right: The Duke of Beaufort pointing out something of interest to his royal guests at the Badminton Horse Trials in 1962. The Queen and her family attend them regularly each April.

Below: A young Prince Charles, in the care of his grandmother and his aunt, leaves Horse Guards after the Trooping the Colour ceremony in June 1951.

The Palace is used for entertaining visiting dignitaries and for state banquets, balls and investitures, which are held in the Ball Room. The Music Room, designed by Nash, is the setting for royal christenings. The Blue Drawing Room, the scene of balls before the present Ball Room was built, has been described as the most beautiful room in the Palace.

Guests at royal garden parties pass through the glass doors of the Bow Room on their way to the Terrace and the gardens. Here they can view the lake and the West Front, the style of which is almost unaltered since George IV's time. The Royal Family's private apartments overlook the gardens flanking Constitution Hill and are on the first floor of the north wing.

The Palace's chapel, bombed in the Second World War, was restored and converted into a unique art gallery in 1961. This is open to the public, as is the Royal Mews, which was designed by John Nash. Now in the care of the Crown Equerry, the Mews houses stables and a number of coaches and carriages which are of great interest, in particular the Gold State Coach built in 1761 for George III and used by the Sovereign at coronations.

The daily routine of monarchy continues, and at 9 a.m. a Scottish piper plays outside the Queen's window, following the tradition begun by Queen Victoria.

On the Thursday before Good Friday the Queen distributes the Royal Maundy Money, the origins of which are lost in the mists of time. Edward the Confessor is said to have initiated the Maundy ceremony during the

A smiling Prince Charles stewarding at Badminton.

eleventh century, though today's version is very different, in that, instead of washing and kissing the feet of the poor, the Queen distributes specially minted alms to as many old men and women as the years of her age. Nowadays the ceremony takes place at Westminster Abbey or one of the provincial cathedrals, often on a date coinciding with an anniversary of their consecration. It is a colourful event, with the Sovereign carrying the traditional nosegay and attended by the Yeomen of the Guard in their scarlet uniforms.

Easter is spent at Windsor Castle, where the annual parade of Boy Scouts takes place in the Quadrangle.

Back in London in June, the Queen goes from Buckingham Palace with members of her family to watch the Derby at Epsom. Their presence helps to make the occasion a notable social event as well as an important day in the racing calendar.

The Queen's personal birthday is 21 April, but she celebrates her official birthday in June with a military parade, the Queen's Birthday Parade, better known as Trooping the Colour. Its origins go back many centuries, but George II was the first monarch to attend the ceremony on Horse Guards Parade, where it is held on the site of the old Palace of Whitehall. The colours trooped are those of a battalion

Right: King George V and Queen Mary in the Garter procession at Windsor in 1913.

Facing page: The Queen at the Trooping the Colour ceremony in 1980. Immediately behind her are the Duke of Edinburgh and Prince Charles.

Below: Prince Charles accompanies his grandmother back to Windsor Castle after the Garter ceremony in 1978.

of one of the five regiments of Foot Guards, accompanied by the massed bands of the Household Cavalry and a Sovereign's escort of either the Life Guards or the Blues and Royals. The Queen rides side-saddle, in military uniform as Colonel-in-Chief of the Household Brigade, and takes the salute accompanied by the royal dukes and colonels of the regiments. The drill is impeccable, orders are kept to the minimum, and a drum beat gives the signal to troop. At the conclusion of the Parade the Queen rides at the head of her Guards along the Mall to Buckingham Palace to take a final salute as they march past, and later, from the balcony, to watch a fly-past.

Sometimes the Birthday Parade does actually coincide with a royal birthday, not the Queen's but that of her husband on 10 June. On a less happy occasion, the death of the Duke of Windsor in 1972, a piper played a special lament in his honour at the Parade.

Summer is a busy time for the Royal Family. The Court returns to Windsor Castle in early June, after the Trooping the Colour ceremony, and on the Monday of Ascot Week another important event takes place. This is the annual service in St George's Chapel for the Knights and Ladies of the Order of the Garter. The investiture of any new Knights of the Order takes place in the Garter Throne Room at Windsor Castle in the morning, followed by a lunch in the Waterloo Chamber. When this is over the Queen and the Knights and Ladies of the Order walk down the staircase to the Grand Entrance, preceded

Top: Watched by her mother, Queen Mary, the Princess Mary picks fruit in Frogmore gardens at Windsor in 1917.

Above: Princess Elizabeth and Princess Margaret taking leading roles in Old Mother Red Riding Boots, *a pantomime staged at Windsor Castle at Christmas 1944.*

Right: King George VI enjoying a ride in Windsor Great Park with his two daughters in 1947.

by the Officers of Arms. There they are met by the Constable and Governor of the Castle, the Military Knights and the Yeomen of the Guard, all of whom join in the procession down the hill to St George's Chapel, making a colourful and intriguing sight. After the special service the Sovereign and her family return up the slope to the Castle in carriages, with the Knights following in cars.

The Order of the Garter is the oldest of its kind in the world, and Garter Day is a particularly happy occasion, said to be England's official birthday.

Windsor Castle, with a history dating back to Norman times, stands, its towers and battlements erect, on a chalk mound twenty-three miles from London, dominating the old town of Windsor below. It was one of a circle of fortresses built by William I around London, and is the oldest of Britain's palaces still in use as a royal home. Very functional, it is still a picturebook building, with the elegance of St George's Chapel at the foot of the hill providing a graceful relief from the sturdy Round Tower at the summit.

Succeeding monarchs have left their marks. Henry VIII built the main gateway bearing his name, while his daughter, Elizabeth I, added what is now the library. Charles II rebuilt the State Apartments, and George III did much to restore the Castle, in which he spent his last unhappy years. It was George IV who dreamed of turning the Castle into a palace to outshine Versailles. The magnificent Waterloo Chamber, actually built in the reign of William IV, was his predecessor's concept, intended to commemorate the defeat of Napoleon by the Duke of Wellington, whose portrait by Thomas Lawrence dominates the room. During the Second World War it was the happy scene of pantomimes enacted by the two Princesses.

The Royal Apartments in the Upper Ward overlook the magnificent gardens, and the

Dressed for one of his riding activities, the Prince of Wales walks on the East Terrace of Windsor Castle with his mother, Prince Edward and the royal corgis in 1969.

Royal Family are able to enjoy riding in Windsor Great Park, where the Duke of Edinburgh practises his four-in-hand carriage driving and the Prince of Wales regularly plays one of his favourite sports, polo.

During Ascot Week the Queen and her houseguests at Windsor often gallop along the racecourse in the early morning, some hours before she and Prince Philip head the procession of open landaus along the straight mile. This is a magnificent sight, the sparkling landaus drawn by Windsor Greys with out-riders and postillions contrasting with the lush green grass and the bright fashion scene. The Royal Family are rightly the centre of attraction for it was at the instigation of Queen Anne that the first Ascot races were run in 1711.

In London the social round continues with a series of garden parties in July at Buckingham Palace, and there is usually one in Scotland, at the Palace of Holyroodhouse in Edinburgh. This is the Queen's official Scottish residence and it dates back to the time of

Left: Helping to make Ascot a royal fashion event.

Below: The Queen and her party watching Henbit win the 1980 Derby at Epsom.

151

Right: Queen Elizabeth and Prince Philip driving down the course at the start of the Royal Ascot meeting in June 1954.

Below: The young Queen and her family watch a polo match at Smith's Lawn, Windsor.

Right: The Queen arrives for Gold Cup Day at Royal Ascot.

Facing page: The Queen greeting a member of her ceremonial bodyguard of the Royal Company of Archers at a garden party at the Palace of Holyroodhouse in Edinburgh in 1978.

James IV of Scotland. It was Mary, Queen of Scots, who made it a royal palace, but the building she knew was largely destroyed in the Civil War when occupied by Cromwell's troops. Charles II began the present palace in 1671, but it was not finally completed until George V's time, though Queen Victoria had already begun the Royal Family's custom of staying there for a few days each year on their way to Balmoral.

Balmoral, on Deeside, is the favourite personal home of the Royal Family, a place where they can relax in privacy in the heart of the Scottish Highlands.

It was in 1842 that Queen Victoria first became enraptured with Scotland, six years later that she rented Balmoral House, eventually buying it in 1853, at which time, with the help of Prince Albert, it was enlarged into a turreted castle. The Balmoral tartan carpets designed by Prince Albert remain, a statue of him in Highland dress dominates the entrance hall, and the joy Queen Victoria took in her Scottish home is still evident.

The Royal Family's 'long holiday' from August until October provides much the same outdoor activities as it did in Queen Victoria's reign. There is sailing and fishing on Loch Muick, picnics and trekking on the moors, shooting, deerstalking and riding. Scottish pipers play daily every morning and after dinner. The Royal Family visit the Highland Games at Braemar, and there is the annual ball for the staff, in which the Queen and her family participate with enthusiasm.

It did not go unnoticed that, long before the royal betrothal was announced in February, Lady Diana Spencer was a guest at Balmoral, and it was to its seclusion that the Prince and his fiancée retreated on his return from his five weeks' overseas tour following

Above: The royal children are shepherded on to a train in 1966. This is the usual mode of transport to Balmoral where the Royal Family have their summer holiday.

Right: An informal photograph of the Royal Family at Balmoral in 1951, with the young Prince Charles pretending to ride a statue.

Left: King George V and Queen Mary driving from Balmoral to morning service at Crathie Church in 1931 accompanied by the Duke and Duchess of York.

Above: Queen Mary, then Duchess of York, at Balmoral with some of her guests. Next to her in the carriage is the Marquise d'Hautpoule and fifth from the left is the composer Tosti.

Left: A gathering of royal relatives at Balmoral. Amongst the guests of the future King Edward VII and Queen Alexandra are Tsar Nicholas II of Russia (second from the right) and the Tsarina (seated centre left).

Right: The Queen and Prince Philip relaxing at Balmoral in 1972.

Below: The eighteen-year-old Prince Charles accompanies the Queen to the State Opening of Parliament for the first time.

Below right: Prince Charles enjoying his toy car at Balmoral in 1952, with the Queen giving him some advice on driving.

Above: The State Opening
of Parliament in 1969.
Prince Charles and Princess
Anne are seated on either
side of their parents in the
House of Lords.

Left: Three royal ladies, the
Queen, her mother and Lady
Sarah Armstrong-Jones,
receive bouquets of heather at
the Braemar Games in 1978.

the formal engagement announcement.

In the autumn the Royal Family return to London, and in November the Queen goes in state to open the new session of Parliament. One of the state ceremonies, it is arranged by the Earl Marshal and the heralds who attend the Sovereign. For the occasion the Queen wears the Imperial State Crown and takes her place of honour in the House of Lords. The blare of a trumpet fanfare is the prelude to her deliverance of the Speech from the Throne, in which the Government's plans for the coming session are announced. The time-honoured ritual, which includes Black Rod knocking on the door of the House of Commons to summon Members to the bar of the House of Lords to hear the Queen's Speech, is part of the tradition of British democracy.

In November the Queen leads the nation's homage to the dead of two world wars by laying a wreath on the Cenotaph in Whitehall on Remembrance Day. This is one of the few occasions, other than state funerals, on which the Queen wears black.

King George V places his wreath on the Cenotaph in Whitehall in memory of the dead of the First World War.

Left: The scene in Whitehall on 9 November 1952 when Queen Elizabeth II laid her first wreath as monarch.

Below left: In 1946 King George VI unveiled a plaque on the Cenotaph to commemorate the dead of the 1939–45 War, thus rededicating the memorial to the dead of two world wars before laying his wreath at its foot.

Below: Remembrance Day 1976. King Olaf of Norway joins the Queen Mother and other members of the Royal Family on a balcony of the Home Office to watch the ceremony in Whitehall.

Right: Prince Charles laying his wreath at the foot of the Cenotaph on Remembrance Day.

Below: Christmas Morning on the steps of St George's Chapel, Windsor. The Queen and other members of the Royal Family exchange greetings after the service.

And so to December and the celebration of Christmas at Windsor Castle. The whole Royal Family gathers to enjoy the festivities in traditional style with Christmas tree. This was first introduced into Britain by Prince Albert in 1841 and has continued in popularity ever since. It is a happy time, with the Queen and her children joining together, young and old alike, to decorate the tree and relax round the glowing log fires. On Christmas morning the members of the Royal Family attend Mattins at St George's Chapel, and the wide steps make a wonderful stage on which to greet the Dean of Windsor and to pause after the service for an exchange of greetings. They return to the Castle for family lunch, and perhaps to watch the Queen's prerecorded Christmas message on television.

The Wedding

For months the preparations had been growing, the excitement mounting, and London was bursting at its seams, its streets gaily decorated. The whole country was en fête for the long-awaited Wedding Day, with houses, streets and gardens festooned with flags and bunting, and pictures of the bride and groom staring down from all sides.

As the youthful Prince of Wales had pledged himself to the service of his country at his Investiture at Caernarvon in 1969, so it was, on 29 July 1981, by his marriage he dedicated himself anew, this time with his bride at his side. It was an event for everyone to enjoy and in which to play his part, from those in high office who were responsible for the ceremonial, those who sewed the beautiful dress of the bride, to those who composed special music in their honour, all happy and, with every act, sending their affectionate good wishes.

It was a magical summer morning on which new beginnings were apparent. The night before Prince Charles had kindled the first of a chain of one hundred and two beacons across the land. That bright, soaring light sent its message to the world, and the cheering that found its echo on the Wedding Day began, rising to a loud crescendo.

Left: A final salute and good wishes for Lady Diana as she leaves Clarence House with her father in the Glass Coach at the start of her journey to St Paul's Cathedral.

Above: Part of the police escort which accompanied the bride to her wedding.

Above: Prince Charles in his State Landau with his brother Prince Andrew, one of his supporters, at his side.

Right: Smiling happily, the Queen and Prince Philip acknowledge the almost deafening cheers of the crowds on their journey to the wedding.

In the bright sunlight, the harness of the escorts jingled, and the carriage processions wound their way to St Paul's. As a commoner, Lady Diana Spencer, veiled, was accompanied by an escort of mounted civil and military police.

The great Cathedral was filled; relatives of the Royal Family, heads of state, friends of the bride and groom, none forgotten by this caring couple, making a mosaic of faces – the colour blending with the magnificent setting of the church on the hill. The moving Service, with new music specially composed, the singing, the fanfare, the simplicity and sincerity of the vows, and the moment of sheer beauty when the bride turned, without her veil, and her radiant face was seen for the first time – remain incapsulated in time's memory. To the cheers and warm affection of thousands, the bride and bridegroom returned to the Palace where, on the balcony, to the ecstatic delight of the throng, they exchanged a kiss.

The last family farewells said, and in a shower of rose petals and confetti, the Prince and Princess of Wales left in a carriage gaily bedecked with blue and silver balloons and a 'Just Married' sign, put there by Prince Andrew and Prince Edward, to catch their train for Romsey to spend the first two days of their honeymoon (as had the Queen and Prince Philip in 1947) in the peace of Broadlands. As the Princess boarded the special train with confetti clinging to her dress, she kissed the Lord Chamberlain, Lord Maclean, farewell, thanking him for all his efforts. Surely that kiss, as had the one on the balcony, emphasized the simplicity and happiness of the Prince and Princess of Wales, and their joy and gratitude was a beacon of hope in the world of 1981. May they have many years of happiness together.

Facing page, left: Mrs Nancy Reagan exchanging a few words with other guests before the ceremony.

Facing page, right: Princess Margaret, her son, Viscount Linley, Princess Anne and Captain Mark Phillips make their way to their seats.

Facing page, bottom: The Lord Mayor of London greeting the bridegroom's parents on their arrival at St Paul's.

Led by the Lord Mayor bearing the Pearl Sword of the City of London, the Queen and Duke of Edinburgh walk down the aisle.

Right: The bride casting an anxious glance at her train.

Below: St Paul's Cathedral, a magnificent setting for a royal wedding.

Above: Lady Sarah Armstrong-Jones and the other bridesmaids adjust Lady Diana's hand-embroidered 25 foot (7·6m) long train as she ascends the red-carpeted steps of the Cathedral.

Centre: On the arm of her father, the bride walks up the long, long aisle to the waiting Prince and the Dean of St Paul's.

Left: The bride and groom before taking their solemn vows. The glorious bouquet of flowers, which included golden Mountbatten roses and the traditional myrtle and veronica, was placed after the wedding on the tomb of the Unknown Warrior in Westminster Abbey.

Above: Earl Spencer giving his daughter in marriage to the Prince of Wales.

Right: Prince Charles and Lady Diana make their marriage vows in a hushed cathedral.

Above: The Archbishop of Canterbury, wearing a new silver cope and mitre for the occasion, blesses the bride and groom after their marriage.

The Prince and Princess of Wales listening to the address by the Archbishop of Canterbury.

The scene in the Cathedral during the ceremony.

Facing page: The Prince has a quiet word with his bride.

172

Facing page: The Archbishop
leads the newly married couple
to the altar for the Prayers.

Left: The Prince and Princess
before the white marble altar.

Right: With the chief bridesmaid, Lady Sarah Armstrong-Jones, in attendance, the bride and groom return from the altar prior to leaving the Cathedral.

The Prince of Wales bows and the Princess of Wales makes her first curtsey to the Queen after their marriage.

Far left: The bridesmaids and pages take up their positions behind the bride and groom.

Left: The bridal procession wends its way down the long aisle, past the smiling faces, to the strains of Elgar's 'Pomp and Circumstance' March No.4.

Right: A view of the bride's dress which shows, to great effect, her train against the red carpet in the aisle.

Above: The service over, their singing finished, the choir leave the Cathedral.

Right: The sight that everyone had been waiting for! The bride and bridegroom on the steps of St Paul's.

Facing page, top: A charming photograph of the bridesmaids in their lovely dresses with pale gold sashes and the pages dressed in the naval cadet uniform of 1863. The bridesmaids were Lady Sarah Armstrong-Jones, India Hicks, Sarah Jane Gaselee, Catherine Cameron and Clementine Hambro. The pages were Lord Nicholas Windsor and Edward van Cutsem.

Facing page, bottom: The Queen and Duke of Edinburgh talking to Princess Margaret and other members of the royal party on the steps of St Paul's after the bride and bridegroom had left the Cathedral.

A smiling Prince and Princess as they pause on the threshold of the Cathedral before getting into their carriage.

Above: Helped by her husband, and watched by the officers and men of the services and regiments in which he served, who acted as step-liners, the Princess of Wales climbs into the 1902 State Postillion Landau.

Right: The Queen pointing out something of interest to Earl Spencer as they return to Buckingham Palace together after the ceremony.

Above: The Duke of Edinburgh driving back along the processional route with the bride's mother, the Hon. Mrs. Shand Kydd.

Left: The carriage bearing the Queen and Earl Spencer driving down Fleet Street.

Far left: Closely guarded by the immaculately accoutred escort, the Prince and Princess of Wales near the end of their journey.

Left: A radiant bride and bridegroom happily acknowledging the cheers of the crowds.

Above: The Princess of Wales, her husband at her side, entering the gates of Buckingham Palace for the first time as third lady in the land. The dense crowds who had waited all night clustered round the Palace to greet them.

Facing page: The kiss on the balcony that says it all. The happy couple embrace to the rapture of the cheering thousands.

Above: The traditional family group on the balcony with the bride and bridegroom, bridesmaids, pages, the Queen and Prince Philip, the Queen Mother, Ruth Lady Fermoy, Prince Andrew, Prince Edward, Earl Spencer and the Hon. Mrs. Shand Kydd.

Left: A close-up of the Prince and Princess of Wales on the balcony with the bridesmaids and pages.

187

Above: The radiant bride in the Spencer family tiara, photographed by the Queen's cousin, Lord Lichfield.

Right: A formal portrait of Prince Charles in the full-dress uniform of Commander of the Royal Navy, and the Princess of Wales in her breathtaking dress designed by David and Elizabeth Emanuel – pure silk ivory taffeta laced with thousands of sequins and pearls, and with a veil of tulle spangled with mother-of-pearl.

The Wedding

Photographic acknowledgments: BIPNA, London 161 right, 162, 166 top left, 168 top, 168 bottom, 171, 172 bottom, 173, 174, 175, 178 – 179, 180 top, 180 bottom, 184 – 185, 185 bottom, 190 – 191; Camera Press, London 166 top right; Tim Graham, London 166 bottom, 169 top, 177 bottom left, 177 bottom right, 178; Patrick Lichfield – Camera Press, London 188 top, 188 bottom, 188 – 189; Press Association, London 167, 168 – 169, 169 bottom, 172 top, 181 top, 181 bottom; Rex Features, London 161 left, 162 – 163, 164 – 165, 170 – 171, 176, 182 top, 182 bottom, 185 top, 186, 187 top, 187 bottom; Syndication International, London 165, 170, 176 – 177, 183 top, 183 bottom.

The photographs used in the royal family tree on page 192 were supplied by Bassano & Vandyk, BIPNA, Hamlyn Group Picture Library, Popperfoto, Syndication International and *The Times*.

Special artwork by Fen Jackson.

The Royal Family wedding group of 1981. The Prince and Princess of Wales with their attendants, the Royal Family, the bride's family and the Crowned Heads of the Royal Families who had come to England for the wedding – Belgium, Norway, Denmark, Sweden, The Netherlands, Luxembourg, Liechtenstein and Monaco – photographed at Buckingham Palace.

Overleaf: Just married! The happy pair leave Buckingham Palace on the first stage of their honeymoon, with the shouts and good wishes of family and friends to speed them on their way.

The Royal House of Windsor: Family Tree

Zara b.1981

Peter b.1977

Princess Anne b.1950 m. Captain Mark Phillips b.1948

Prince Andrew b.1960

Charles Prince of Wales b.1948 m. Lady Diana Spencer b.1961

Prince Edward b.1964

Sarah b.1964

David Viscount Linley b.1961

Richard Duke of Gloucester b.1944 m. Birgitte van Deurs b.1946

Prince William 1941-72

Elizabeth II b.1926 Queen 1952- m. Philip Duke of Edinburgh b.1921

Princess Margaret b.1930 m. Antony Armstrong-Jones Earl of Snowdon b.1930 div.1978

Edward Duke of Kent b.1935 m. Katharine Worsley b.1933

Henry Duke of Gloucester 1900-74 m Lady Alice Montagu-Douglas-Scott b.1901

Edward VIII Duke of Windsor 1894-1972 King 1936 m. Wallis Simpson b.1896

George VI 1895-1952 King 1936-52 m. Lady Elizabeth Bowes-Lyon b.1900

George Duke of Kent 1902-42 m. Marina Princess of Greece 1906-68

Princess Alexandra b.1936 m. Hon. Angus Ogilvy b.1928

Prince Michael b.1942 m. Marie-Christine von Reibnitz b.1945

Louis Earl Mountbatten of Burma 1900-79 m. Hon. Edwina Ashley 1901-60

Alice of Battenberg 1885-1969 m. Andrew of Greece 1882-1944

George V 1865-1936 King 1910-36 m. Mary of Teck 1867-1953

Mary Princess Royal 1897-1965 m. 6th Earl of Harewood 1882-1947

George 7th Earl of Harewood b.1923

Victoria of Hesse 1863-1950 m. Louis of Battenberg (later Mountbatten) 1854-1921

Princess Alice 1843-78 m. Louis IV of Hesse 1837-92

Edward VII 1841-1910 King 1901-10 m. Alexandra of Denmark 1844-1925

Alfred Duke of Edinburgh (Duke of Saxe-Coburg & Gotha) 1844-1900

Helena Princess Christian of Schleswig-Holstein 1846-1923

Victoria Princess Royal 1840-1901

Beatrice Princess Henry of Battenberg 1857-1944

Leopold Duke of Albany 1853-84

Victoria 1819-1901 Queen 1837-1901 m. Albert of Saxe-Coburg & Gotha 1819-61

Arthur Duke of Connaught 1850-1942

Louise Duchess of Argyll 1848-1939